# MORGAN THREE-WHEELER

## STEPHEN CLARK

AMBERLEY

*Front cover, top*: A 1921 Grand Prix model revisits its birthplace a hundred years after the Pickersleigh Road factory opened in 1914. (Richard Atherton); *bottom*: The same car at the Firle Hillclimb on the South Downs in 2016. (Gun Hill Studios)

*Back cover*: A 2023 Super 3 at Goodwood. (Author)


First published 2024

Amberley Publishing
The Hill, Stroud,
Gloucestershire, GL5 4EP

www.amberley-books.com

ISBN: 978 1 3981 1811 9 (print)
ISBN: 978 1 3981 1812 6 (ebook)

British Library Cataloguing in Publication Data.
A catalogue record for this book is available from the British Library.

Typeset in 10pt on 13pt Celeste.
Origination by Amberley Publishing.
Printed in the UK.

'It's the old adage . . .
The more you put into something,
the more you get out of it'

# Contents

# Acknowledgements

The author wishes to thank the following for their invaluable help towards producing this book: Jake Alderson, Richard Atherton, Christian Baker, Chris Booth, Brands Hatch Morgans, Gordon Button, Sue Clark, Tom Cowley, Ken Ellis, Brian Galbraith, Grahame Joseph, Paul Jowitt, Wendy Kingshott, Ken Kiss, John Larkham, Steve Lister, June and John Macara, Joris Mans, Arnold Marshall, Graham Murrell, Steve Nash, Rhys Nolan, Mandy Pachol, Dave Pittuck, Roy Plummer, Sam Savage, Alan Sharpe, V-Twin, Andy Warren, Martyn Webb, Alain Wilczynski and Angela Williams.

Sincere thanks are also due to the following for permission to use copyright material in this book: Crystal Palace Museum, the Francis Frith Collection, Gun Hill Studios, the Morgan Family, Morgan Motor Company, the Morgan Three-Wheeler Club.

Every attempt has been made to seek permission for copyright material used in this book. If copyright material has been inadvertently used without permission or acknowledgement, the necessary correction will be made at the first opportunity, with apologies.

# Introduction

Fuel on; tickle the float; oil on – and visibly dripping through the dashboard sight-glass en route to the engine; ignition on; air, magneto advance/retard and throttle levers set; decompressor lever raised; a flick of the starting handle and the big V-twin rumbles and spits into life; wriggle in behind the wheel and lower goggles. These are the preliminaries to one of life's more exhilarating experiences: an outing in a Morgan three-wheeler. The vintage Morgan's nine-point starting procedure is much simplified in its modern descendant, but, whichever car, a similarly thrilling and memorable motoring adventure awaits.

In 1909 H. F. S. Morgan perfected his design for an economical and inexpensive runabout. Light but strong, with two wheels in front and one behind, it was powered by a hefty V-twin motorcycle engine mounted well to the fore. Power was transmitted by shaft to the gears astern whence chains drove the single rear wheel. Four-cylinder Ford car engines were fitted to new models from 1934, but the basic configuration remained unchanged until, through lack of demand, the three-wheelers were discontinued in 1952. Sixty years later the Morgan Motor Company reprised the same formula with the inspired re-introduction of the three-wheeler to their range in 2012. The new M3W's traditional looks were more akin to the pre-Ford-era cars, having reverted to a big, exposed V-twin engine and beetleback styling, but the technology was strictly twenty-first century, with performance to match. In 2022 the company further demonstrated its faith in the future of the three-wheeler by replacing the M3W with the Super 3, featuring monocoque construction, three-cylinder Ford power and even more verve.

Thanks to inherently clever design providing economy, reliability and high performance, coupled with a sensible range of models, the three-wheeled Morgan has enjoyed a successful, albeit lengthily interrupted career for well over a hundred years. Total production has not yet exceeded 25,000 – modest indeed compared with twelvefold Austin Seven numbers – and yet the little cars' reputation and popularity are formidable, worldwide and ever-growing. On the move a Morgan three-wheeler will stir normally sober bystanders into smiles and manic gesticulation, while parked up it will draw a crowd within minutes.

For those who have yet to relish that life-changing first drive, this book may scratch the itch a little until their time comes. For the already initiated, I hope it will provide interesting and entertaining reading.

Morgans had their serious side too. Here, Police Sergeant Holland and 'Bob' patrol the Gloucester streets in a late 1920s Standard model. (Alderson collection)

# CHAPTER 1

# Pre-Morgan Britain

## Victorian Motoring

Consider the motoring scene in Great Britain at the turn of the twentieth century when Harry Morgan, a nineteen-year-old engineering student, was taking a serious interest in the design of bicycles, motorcycles and motor cars.

As recently as 1895 there had been fierce institutional opposition to the motor car. The horse as a means of transport, it was maintained, was very much alive and kicking and the motoring craze would be short-lived; the advance of the motor car was a noisy, dangerous threat to society and should be suppressed; the French obsession with motoring was typical Continental silliness. Such backward-looking views were in decline by 1900, but there were still fewer than 20,000 cars on the road here – mostly imported models owned by wealthy hobby drivers. The idea of the motor car as a means of practical, everyday transport had not yet been embraced.

Across the Channel, the French, *au contraire*, were already hugely enthusiastic motorists, private and state support having been lavished on the movement from its infancy. They were at the dawn of a major new industry – possibly ten years ahead of us. Manufacturers such as Panhard, Peugeot and de Dion-Bouton were already well-established and flourishing. The spectacular and dramatic inter-city road races that had been staged since the 1880s had fired the Gallic imagination to the extent that, although ownership of a motor car was beyond the pocket of the average Frenchman, he was nevertheless an aspiring *automobiliste*.

With an eye to these developments, various luminaries such as S. F. Edge and Sir David Salomons saw the possibilities for British industry. They organised motor exhibitions to whet the public appetite with currently available models and demonstrate the real possibilities of motor transport. In 1896 pressure from the pro-motoring lobby resulted in new legislation which lifted our archaic speed limit from 4 to 14mph (it was raised again to 20mph in 1903) and removed the requirement for a red-flag-bearing vanguard. A 1,000-mile trial was run in 1900 in which sixty-five cars of mostly British and French build toured a route around Britain from London to Edinburgh and back, punctuated by motor exhibitions in various cities along the way. That year James Gordon-Bennett, an American newspaper tycoon, launched his prestigious annual long-distance international road race to encourage manufacturers worldwide to help break French domination of the industry. Napier and Wolseley rose to that challenge, while other pioneer British car makers such as Daimler, Humber, Lanchester and Vauxhall were soon producing passenger cars in some numbers.

The 1,000 Mile Trial started from Grosvenor Place, London, on 23 April 1900 alongside Queen Victoria's rather forbidding garden wall. (*The Autocar*)

Illustrious racer Charles Jarrott clings to his Wolseley in the 1904 Gordon-Bennett Cup race, staged in Germany. Portrait by Leslie Ward (Spy), *c.* 1905. (Author's collection)

# Edwardian Motoring and the Cyclecar

In 1900 Harry was a promising student at the Crystal Palace School of Practical Engineering. He would soon display a canny business sense, too. Perhaps, even as he cycled through the Sydenham horse traffic from his lodgings to the school, he foresaw imminent opportunities for mass motorised transport.

By 1905 the powerful luxury motor car, staple of the industry, had reached a standard form that would remain largely unchanged for twenty-five years. At the lower end, however, there were few products to suit growing demand. Tricars and forecars, relics from the 1890s, had become increasingly complex, heavy and expensive, offering neither weather protection nor civilised accommodation. De Dion-type motor tricycles were popular and relatively cheap, but by their nature were limited in their usefulness. French and British *voiturettes*, admirable little scaled-down versions of grander siblings, were well-built and reliable with 'sociable' seating, but shelter from the elements was minimal and, at £200 to £300, they were not cheap. Motorcycles and combinations had come of age and could be bought for under £100, but the riding experience was often cold, wet and primitive.

The Crystal Palace School of Practical Engineering occupied three floors of the Palace's 284-foot cast-iron-framed South Tower, viewed here from Westow Hill, South Norwood, in 1898. (Copyright the Francis Frith Collection)

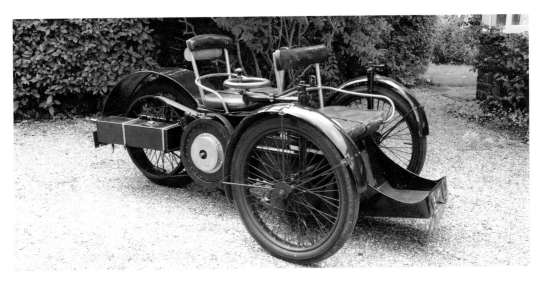

The first Léon Bollée 'Voiturette' was a tricar; this is an 1896 example. (Author)

Charles Jarrott again – this time seen riding his De Dion tricycle en route from Paris to Bordeaux in the 1899 race. (Author's collection)

None of these options was entirely satisfactory. The man on the Clapham omnibus sought a small, reliable runabout for travelling to work during the week and amusing his family at weekends. It should be cheap to run and cheap to buy – under £100 – and protect its occupants from the worst of the weather. The major car makers showed little interest in developing such vehicles, so it was left to lone pioneering engineers, often in sheds, to respond to the call. It is generally acknowledged that Harry Morgan's was the first serious offering to emerge in 1909, but the GN and the French Bédélia appeared almost simultaneously. It is unlikely that, as he put the finishing touches to his prototype in Malvern, Harry had any notion that he was at the threshold of the cyclecar revolution – indeed the term 'cyclecar' had not yet been coined. Nor could he have imagined that he had perfected what was to be the most successful and long-lived example of that breed.

Prompted by Harry's decision to exhibit his Runabout at the first International Cycle and Motorcycle Exhibition at Olympia in 1910 and the euphoric publicity it generated, there was an explosion of new ideas, designs, models and manufacturers. By 1913 the number of makers in this country had expanded from a handful to over a hundred, though many of them were blacksmith-grade engineers producing crude, if not downright dangerous contraptions based on dubious design principles. Wooden chassis, wire-and-bobbin steering, fore-and-aft sliding axles to engage or slacken drive belts and fragile fibreboard bodywork were all commonplace.

The best examples relied mostly on motorcycle components with, typically, a proprietary single-cylinder or V-twin engine sitting in a tube-and-lug frame delivering power via clutched gears and chain or belt drive. Differentials were seldom needed on the generally narrow, four-wheeled cars. Bodywork was skimpy, usually accommodating two people side by side or in tandem. Braking was vestigial. The cars were cheap and popular and by 1912 the 'Cyclecar Movement' or 'New Motoring' was in full swing. The Austin Seven was at least ten years away, so for the time being, as far as budget motoring was concerned, cyclecars would have to do.

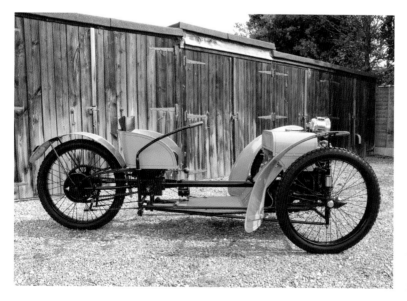

H. F. S. Morgan's 1909 prototype Morgan is perfectly recreated in this replica. (Author)

# CHAPTER 2

# Some Morgan History

The Morgan story is as much about strong family values as it is about cars. Harry Morgan was the undisputed architect of the three-wheeled runabout that was to make his name, but it is unlikely that talent and tenacity alone would have sustained him without the generous and unstinting support of his parents – particularly that of his remarkable father, Henry George Morgan. Later on, Harry would be equally supportive of succeeding generations.

## H. G. Morgan

Harry's father 'HG' was born in 1852 to a wealthy family whose ecclesiastical connections stretched back for well over a century. They lived in Nunhead, South-East London, where HG's father, also Henry Morgan, was chaplain to the vast cemetery there. HG, an only child, was educated at nearby Dulwich College prior to his inevitable training and career as a parson.

In 1871, at the age of seventy-three, Henry Sr purchased the living of Stoke Lacey in the diocese of Hereford where he became rector. Installed in the fine rectory, whose 19-acre curtilage encompassed landscaped gardens and an extensive range of cottages and outbuildings, he and his family lived in some style. HG and his sweetheart Florence, who had met as neighbours in the Nunhead days, were married in 1875 and set up home in the marginally less grand New House in the nearby village of Moreton Jeffries. Following his ordination in 1877, HG worked first as curate at Stoke Lacey and then as vicar of Moreton Jeffries from 1884 until his father's death in 1886 when he inherited the living and the rectory at Stoke Lacey. He occupied both, as the devout and much-loved rector, until his death in 1936.

HG's and Florence's first child, Henry Frederick Stanley – Harry – was born in 1881, followed by a daughter, Frieda, in 1882. Their second son, Charles George, arrived in 1884 but lived for only three years – a loss that doubtless led to a special bond between HG and Harry. The birth of two more daughters, Ethel and Dorothy, completed a loving and happy family.

*Above left*: H. F. S. Morgan's grandparents and father, 'HG', in 1876. (Morgan family albums)

*Above right*: A much-loved rector, H. G. Morgan, *c.* 1910. (Morgan family albums)

Early in their marriage Florence inherited substantial family legacies. HG set about managing this supplementary wealth and soon showed himself to be a naturally skilled investor and stock-market player. By the time they returned to Stoke Lacey the Morgans had accumulated a considerable fortune and were enjoying a privileged lifestyle. Later, HG's exceptional financial acumen and sound commercial thinking would be fundamental to his son's business.

At first sight, a stern Victorian gentleman emerges from contemporary photographs of the tall, frock-coated, top-hatted HG, but on closer study there is a twinkle in the eye and a chuckle around the mouth beneath the snowy whiskers which betray affability and kindliness. Talented and popular, he was, despite outward appearances, a man with modern interests and attitudes and a fascination for the technological developments of his time.

In an age when parents tended to impose professions on their children, HG's enlightened ideas were unorthodox. In time he acknowledged Harry's pronounced leaning towards engineering and, abandoning any further notions of a career in the Church, allowed him free rein. In all Harry's activities, from his education to the financing and running of his enterprises, HG and Florence were intelligently, generously and unconditionally supportive.

# H. F. S. Morgan

Harry and his sisters spent idyllic and privileged childhoods at Stoke Lacey rectory. Aged ten, having been tutored at home for some years, Harry was sent to a small preparatory boarding school, Stone House, in Broadstairs. The shock must have been profound. For a shy, quite frail child from a gentle and genteel background, the challenges of overcoming homesickness and finding acceptance in that tough environment would have been daunting. Nevertheless, his copious letters home suggest that he remained cheerful and buoyant, and that life was at least tolerable. Perhaps his fertile imagination provided escape during difficult times.

Harry did not thrive at Stone House. He shone in maths and art and in the workshops but was otherwise weak in academic subjects – or was just bored by them. It was clear, though, from his prolific sketches of boats, trains and motors, where his real interests lay. In 1894 he failed the exam for entry to Eton so his father, nursing a vain hope that a Church career might still be in the offing, sent him to Marlborough, then traditionally a school for the sons of clergymen. Harry fared even worse there and HG, conceding defeat, removed him in favour of a broader, arts-based education at home, on European tours with the family and finally, for a few months, at a new, small school in Clifton, Bristol.

It was now plain to Harry's parents that his passion for engineering was no passing whim, so they began to focus their efforts on preparing him for his preferred career. A place was secured for him at the Crystal Palace School of Practical Engineering, housed in the Palace's colossal, Brunel-designed South Tower in Sydenham, South London. At last Harry was in his element. The quality of training offered by the School was first class, and in 1899 he embarked on his course with relish. Specialising in mechanical engineering, design and technical drawing, he passed all subjects with flying colours two years later, having also enjoyed free access to state-of-the-art workshops to develop his own projects.

The Crystal Palace School of Practical Engineering in 1873. (Crystal Palace Museum)

15

To complete Harry's engineering credentials, HG underwrote an apprenticeship for him at the Swindon works of the Great Western Railway, starting in 1901. A pupillage under GWR's chief mechanical engineer G. J. Churchward was a prestigious and enviable training. Harry received meticulous instruction in all disciplines of the profession, but he ultimately favoured design. By the end of 1904 he had served his time and was equipped for work.

At Swindon Harry had become an enthusiastic, sometimes madcap motorist firstly on an 8hp Eagle Tandem tri-car bought from the spoils of his twenty-first birthday in 1902, later replaced by a 7hp Little Star. Returning fully qualified to Stoke Lacey, he discussed his ambitions with his father. He wanted to establish his own motor business, a proposal which HG was more than happy to support both financially and paternally. In early 1905 Harry bought Chestnut Villa, Worcester Road, Malvern Link – 15 miles from Stoke Lacey. In partnership with Leslie Bacon, an old friend and recently qualified engineer, he built and equipped an imposing 2,800sqft garage on an adjoining site and opened for business in May as Morgan & Co., offering a complete range of services for the motorist and with agencies for the sales of Darracq, Wolseley and Siddeley cars.

After some years of prosperous trading, Harry's fertile brain turned to the design of a small single-seater car. W. J. Stephenson-Peach, a family friend and the distinguished engineering

Madcap. HFS on his Eagle Tandem at Stoke Lacey Rectory in 1904. A future design influence? (Morgan Motor Co.)

The new, eye-catching garage in Worcester Road, Malvern Link, in 1905. By 1910 the exuberant signage had disappeared and the business of building Morgans was being carried on in earnest behind obscured windows. (Morgan Motor Co.)

master at Malvern College, was enthusiastic. Pooling their ideas and using the College's well-equipped workshops, they completed a three-wheeled, Peugeot-engined prototype in 1909. Tests were so successful that Harry decided to gauge the commercial appeal of the project at Olympia's 1910 International Cycle and Motor Cycle Exhibition. On the strength of a few orders an area of the garage was set aside for the cars' assembly. Wary of the financial risk involved in manufacturing, Leslie Bacon withdrew from the partnership at this point.

Interest in the first single-seater, tiller-steered Morgans was encouraging, but did not translate into many sales orders until 1911 when the two-seater, wheel-steered cars were launched. Demand rose quickly and the entire garage was soon devoted to runabout production. The Morgan three-wheeler had properly arrived.

In 1912 Harry married Ruth Day, a vivacious vicar's daughter whom he had met at a dance five years before. She was the perfect foil for the shy, reserved entrepreneur and partnered him in countless trials in Morgans over the ensuing years. They raised their five children in Chestnut Villa, moving to the grander Fern Lodge nearby in 1925, and finally, in 1935, to Cannon Hill, a fine mansion and estate in Bray, Berkshire.

Harry masterminded the design and development of Morgan cars throughout the period up to the Second World War, including the transition from three to four wheels which was so vital to the marque's survival. He also campaigned his cars in competition widely and successfully throughout this time to promote their great merits to the public.

In 1935, coinciding with the move to Bray, he reduced his immediate involvement with the factory to one day per week, enjoying the rest of his retirement with his family, his estate and his fine cars. He died in 1959 aged seventy-seven.

## Morgan Motor Co. Ltd

The possibility of their sapling enterprise growing fast into a major manufacturing concern, with all the accompanying financial implications, prompted Harry – henceforth referred to as HFS – and his father to set the business on a more formal footing. On 1 April 1912, Morgan Motor Co. Ltd was formed with a nominal share capital of £100,000, HG as chairman and HFS as managing director. It is not clear to what extent the shares were paid up but both father and son invested substantially. HG and HFS took responsibility, respectively, for the company and the cars.

Throughout HFS's lifetime and beyond, the company's success and survival were founded on HG's astute and cautious financial principles: borrowing was avoided; mass-production, involving heavy capital investment and loss of flexibility, was never contemplated; assembly of bought-in components rather than full-scale manufacture was preferred; cars were only built to order – none went into stock; capital projects were financed from the company's own funds; large built-up reserves were held in the form of investments whose income supported the company through lean years.

Demand for Morgan runabouts escalated. The Worcester Road garage was extended to its rearward limits, but by 1913 orders had reached a level where the now seventy-man workforce was struggling to fulfil them in the available space. At the end of the year a 2-acre plot was acquired, half a mile away, in Pickersleigh Road, Malvern. The opening of a new, two-bay factory building in the summer of 1914 collided with the outbreak of the First World War. That building was not fully operational until 1919.

In the early years work at Worcester Road was limited to constructing the tubular chassis and wooden body frames, machining, upholstery, painting and final assembly. Engines, castings, bevel boxes and tinwork were all bought in, but body panels were made on the premises later. From 1914 rolling chassis and panelled bodies were transported from Worcester Road to Pickersleigh Road to be conjoined, painted and trimmed, ready for despatch.

The war forced Morgan to put its growth plan on hold and curtail existing activities. Demand fell, orders were cancelled, and many workers joined the conflict. Dwindling production was prohibited altogether after 1916, but profitable munitions contracts enabled the company to keep the factory running and generate funds to complete and properly equip the Pickersleigh Road buildings for the resumption of motor assembly in 1919. At that time two further bays were added, followed by two more in 1922. By 1929 a seventh and final bay had been built at Pickersleigh Road and production was fully disengaged from the old Worcester Road works. By now Morgan was employing 150 men. The same factory buildings, expanded and modernised, house the company today.

Shyness, rather than aloofness, made HFS a somewhat distant figure on the factory floor. He preferred to confer with his works manager, Alfie Hales, than mix directly with the workforce. He had met and been impressed by Hales in 1906 and quickly recruited him to run the garage. A no-nonsense Brummie, Hales was a natural practical engineer, and mutual respect soon developed between the two men. Later, he was an obvious choice to manage the factory, and despite being sometimes volatile and high-handed, he was popular with the men. Alfie died, prematurely and much lamented, in 1927, to be replaced by George Goodall, a local man who was later, in 1937, appointed managing director after HFS had stepped up as chairman on his father's death.

Car production was suspended for the duration of the Second World War when, once again, the factory diverted its much-diminished resources to helping the war effort.

Following the death of HFS in 1959, the company was run first by his son, Peter, and then his grandson, Charles, until 2013. It remained in Morgan family ownership until 2019 when a majority holding was acquired by Investindustrial, a global private equity firm.

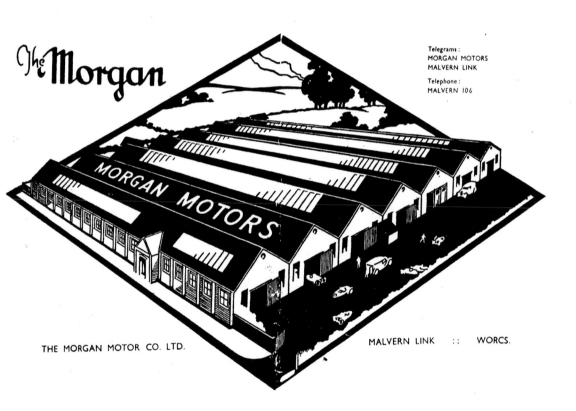

A stylised view of the Pickersleigh Road factory in 1935. (Morgan Motor Co.)

# CHAPTER 3

# How Morgans Work

There is a common misconception that the Morgan chassis was made of wood. No, no, NO! This is pure myth. It is true that a few of the earlier, more primitive cyclecars were thus constructed – probably through their makers' lack of metalwork skills – but the Morgan was never among them.

By the accepted method of motor car assembly in 1910, a coach-built body was fixed to the rails of a cast-iron or fabricated-steel chassis at multiple points. Coach building involved forming aluminium or sheet-steel panels around the shape of a complex but light, generally ash-made, frame to make a body which had little inherent strength until it was firmly bolted to its partner, the chassis. The resultant union became the reasonably rigid structure required for adequate road behaviour. Regardless of the efficacy of its suspension, the chassis of a four-wheeled car is subjected to torsion under certain driving conditions, the resultant stresses being transmitted to the body and eventually causing damage in the form of cracked panels and loose joinery.

The Morgan did not follow those conventions. The tubular, triangulated frame was light and strong, and the body had inherent stiffness, being a wooden box or tub incorporating the floor and bulkheads, with steel panels fixed externally. Once united, body and chassis formed a rigid and robust entity and the three-wheel configuration ensured that, like the Milkmaid's Stool, negligible torsional stress was suffered (loose joints and metal fatigue were, instead, caused by engine vibration). All pre-1939 V-twin Morgans were built in this fashion.

Meanwhile the F-Type, introduced in 1933, returned to traditional methods just as mainstream car makers were experimenting with unitary construction and discarding the chassis altogether. The F-Type body was a more flexible, coach-built affair which sat on the rails of a fabricated, Z-section pressed-steel chassis. That arrangement continued unchanged until three-wheelers were dropped completely by Morgan in 1952, though four-wheelers were built along very similar lines well into the twenty-first century.

The 2012 M3W bore closer resemblance to the V-twin cars than to the later F-Types and the similarity ran more than skin deep, the M3W chassis being of tubular construction. The detailed chassis design of the modern car was, however, quite different, with larger diameter tubes forming a rigid spaceframe that surrounded the occupants with some degree of protection from mishap. The body was coach built with an aluminium-panelled ash frame.

Morgan has severed all lingering connections with Edwardian technology in the Super 3. Gone is the coach building, gone the tubed chassis frame. Instead, they have used a bonded aluminium monocoque with stressed, super-formed body panels to create the body/chassis. Engine, suspension, bevel box and steering are mounted on complex, multipurpose aluminium castings, which also add rigidity to the structure.

## Two-Speeders

Examine the frame of any old British motorcycle. The chances are that it is constructed from an assortment of shaped steel tubes brazed into cast-iron connectors or 'lugs'. Additional lugs slide onto the tubes to provide mountings for the engine, suspension, pedals and other ancillaries. The first production Morgan chassis, now known as the Narrow B, followed this pattern in 1910 and changed little in the ensuing three decades.

The bronze, rear-mounted bevel box – in essence a rudimentary gearbox – was at the heart of the chassis and was integral to it. Two 1in (1¼in from 1913) tubes ran from either side of the box to the front of the car where they formed the lower engine mountings (and doubled as exhaust pipes well into the 1920s). Above them a 2in (2¼in from 1922) central torque tube was soldered into the bevel box and ran forwards at engine crankshaft level, terminating in a cruciform assembly, which provided the upper engine and body mountings and formed a space for the cone clutch and flywheel. Two parallel 1in cross-tubes were joined, one above the other and 12in apart, at right-angles to the upper cruciform and lower main tubes. They were linked at their outer ends by steel pillars on which bronze, coil-sprung stub-axle assemblies could slide – vertically to provide independent suspension and rotationally for steering.

At the rear, a cross-tube linking the two lower main tubes passed through the bevel box and gave it support. Two angle-irons, bolted laterally to the top of the box, provided mounting points for the rear, quarter-elliptic leaf-springs and the body tub. The rear wheel fork, fabricated from a cast-iron web, two 1in tubes (later 1⅛in) and forged fork-ends, pivoted in the lower bevel box casing.

A flywheel and cone clutch assembly were mounted externally on the rear engine main-shaft. Early clutches engaged metal-to-metal but were later leather – and from 1917, Ferodo-lined. Power was transmitted thence by a north/south propshaft running through the torque tube to the bevel box where a pair of robust bevel gears reduced revolutions by a factor of two-and-a-half and diverted them to an east/west-oriented counter-shaft.

The two-speed final drive was a model of simplicity. High- and low-speed sprockets ran freely on the counter-shaft to the left and right, respectively, of the bevel box. Chains ran thence to sprockets on either side of the rear wheel. By means of sliding dog-clutches, controlled by a lever next to the driver's right knee, one or other pair of sprockets could be locked into drive while its partner was left to free-wheel. A central position, where no dogs meshed, gave neutral.

The year 1921 brought some refinements to the Narrow B: the clutch withdrawal mechanism was improved, redesigned fork-ends enabled easier extraction of the rear wheel

Rear end of the 1925 two-speeder chassis. (Morgan Motor Co.)

Front end of the 1925 two-speeder chassis. (Morgan Motor Co.)

without removing the chains, and revised sprocket ratios meant that equal-length, thus interchangeable, chains could be used.

The Wide B chassis of 1926 carried a wider, stronger bevel box and a modified cruciform layout, but the first major revision to the B came in 1929 with the M chassis, in which the whole rear assembly, comprising bevel box, fork, springs, chains and wheel, was detachable from the chassis, affording greatly improved access for maintenance. A stronger, forged fork assembly pivoted around the bevel box counter-shaft to provide constant chain tension, and underslung springs gave a lower centre of gravity. The 1931 C-variant chassis, designed for the Sports Family model, was 4in longer and incorporated a two-part propshaft supported by a bearing at its joint which eliminated whip. (This became, essentially, the chassis used in the three-speeders.)

19in × 2½in beaded-edge-type, non-detachable wire wheels were superseded in the early 1920s by well-type rims. Brakes were confined to the rear wheel where two 5½in drums were incorporated either side of the hub, the foot pedal operating a Ferodo-lined contracting band on the right and an externally mounted hand lever carrying out the same work to the left. The right-hand drum was enlarged to 6½in in 1921. Internally expanding 6in front wheel drum brakes arrived as an optional extra in 1923. These were operated independently of the rear wheel, via a system of compensating cables, by a ratcheted lever assembly clamped to the torque tube. They became standard equipment in 1927 with 7in drums.

Crank-starting was performed at the lower, rear driver's side of the car where the handle, inserted through a hole in the bodywork, connected with the counter-shaft. The bevel box converted one turn of the handle to two-and-a-half of the engine, so a decompressor lever was sited on the outer cockpit side to ease rapid spinning of the engine and prevent driver exhaustion and shoulder damage. Electric self-starters, operating on a flywheel ring, were optional from 1924.

The very early cars' tiller steering was outdated by mid-1911 when it was replaced by direct wheel steering, which was fitted until 1927. This worked well on the move, but was so heavy during parking manoeuvres that it paid to ask a pedestrian assistant to manually swivel the wheels in the required direction to avoid straining the mechanism. A 2:1 reduction box was available as an extra in 1928 and was standardised in 1929. Engine throttle, air and ignition control levers were mounted on the steering wheel, though a foot throttle could be specified at extra cost.

The early optional acetylene lighting equipment was more effective than the modern-but-dim 6V Lucas lighting set, which was offered in 1915, standardised in 1926 and continued to cast its pool of gloom ahead of Morgans right up to 1952. Dynamos were belt-driven from a flywheel pulley until 1926, after which they were rear-mounted and gear-driven from the bevel box counter-shaft. Early batteries sat on the running board and were later moved behind the seats. Many surviving Morgans have been converted to 12V systems for safety.

## Three-Speeder Twins

Aside from a new range of engines, there was little, externally, to differentiate a new 1932 three-speeder from its two-speed predecessor. An updated version of the two-speeder

C-variant chassis, with its two-part propshaft and supporting bearing, was now adopted as standard equipment. The torque tube, enlarged to 2½in diameter, was fitted with a modified lug to mate with the conventional new Burman-type three-speed-and-reverse gearbox and accommodate the selector rods, which connected the now centrally mounted gear lever. The R gearbox – lubricated by Castrol R – was prone to overheating and was fitted in 1932 only. It was modified unsuccessfully and replaced with the D version – lubricated by Castrol D – the following year. Chassis were designated R and D after their respective gearboxes. A single plate clutch replaced the old cone device and a lone chain, on the driver's side, drove the rear wheel. The sporting models had slightly taller gear ratios. All three-speeders were fitted with self-starters. Crank-starting was not possible through the gearbox as before, so the new engines had provision for a handle at the front.

In 1933, when the transition from two- to three-speeders was complete, detachable 18in × 3in Dunlop Magna wheels were fitted and the drop in the front cross-tubes was standardised at 1in. After this the cars remained, in essence, unchanged until their demise. Even after thirty years of continuous development, HFS's original design was still entirely recognisable at the heart of the last V-twin cars built in 1939.

D-type chassis of a 1934 three-speeder Super Sports, complete with JAP LTOWZ. The gearbox-driven alternator is a modern concession. (Tom Cowley)

# F-Types

Sets of lugs for the V-twin chassis were cast in a local foundry. Once machined at the Morgan factory, it was a straightforward matter to braze them onto the relevant tubes to create a frame. The Ford-engined cars, however, launched in 1933, were built on an entirely new, pressed-steel chassis, the complexities of which made in-house fabrication unviable. Manufacture was delegated to Rubery Owen in nearby Darlaston, who, incidentally, continued to produce Morgan chassis until the late 1970s.

Two Z-section side rails were joined at the rear by a pair of channel-section cross-members that supported the gearbox and quarter-elliptic springs. Further forward, the rails were linked behind the engine by a Z-section cross-member and, at the front, by a tubular cross-head assembly similar to the V-twin cars. The vertical sliding-axle suspension was also retained. The various elements were either bolted or riveted together. The familiar central torque tube, now running level with the side rails, connected to the gearbox, as before, with a lug but was soldered at the front into the engine bell-housing, itself bolted to the Z-section cross-member and enclosing the flywheel and clutch assembly. The upper, outward-facing flanges of the Z-section rails provided an effective platform on which to mount the body, while the lower inward-facing flanges nicely accommodated the floor-boards.

A water-cooled 8hp or 10hp four-cylinder Ford engine sat, rigidly fixed, between the front chassis rails and behind the front axle line. Rearwards of the bell-housing, which enclosed a flywheel and single plate clutch, transmission was almost identical to the V-twins, but the gearbox had slightly shorter ratios.

Much of the running gear was inherited from the V-twins. Dunlop Magnas remained and braking arrangements were similar except all three wheels now operated in unison from the foot pedal while the central ratchet lever worked a rear parking brake. Steering

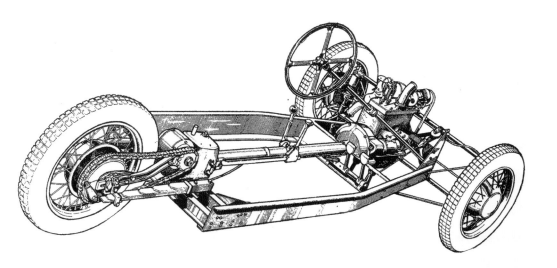

F-type chassis. (*Light Car*)

was geared down 2:1 as before but the track-rod and drag-link were now sited in front of the axle line. The usual engine controls on the steering wheel were supplemented by a foot throttle and 6V electrics were retained.

## Morgan Three-Wheeler

Apart from the ash body frames, which were made at the Morgan factory, the major elements of the M3W – engine, chassis, body panels, suspension, brakes, steering, cush-drive, gearbox, and bevel box were manufactured by external suppliers.

A complex, robust box/ladder chassis-frame of 1½in round-section tube was at the core. This was enclosed by an aluminium-panelled, coach-built body. The 2-litre, air-cooled S&S V-twin engine was mounted in front of the axle line in traditional style. A cush-drive fitted between engine and flywheel/clutch assembly protected the five-speed Mazda MX5 gearbox from the S&S's destructive torque. A propshaft continued rearwards through a tunnel to a Quaife bevel box, which converted drive from north/south to east/west as in the two-speeders. Final drive was by a toothed belt running between toothed pulleys on the bevel box and rear wheel.

An early M3W chassis frame. From 2014 the engine bay was strengthened with welded, triangulating support tubes to alleviate cracking problems. (Andrew Warren)

The S&S Wedge engine, cush-drive housing and Mazda gearbox of the M3W. (Andrew Warren)

Front suspension was by double wishbones with semi-outboard coil springs while the coil-sprung rear wheel was fixed between swinging arms. The skinny 19in × 3in front wire wheels were fitted with 10½in disc brakes and the wide, 16in alloy rear carried a 9in drum. Steering was by rack and pinion mounted behind the engine.

## Super 3

HFS's elegant engineering style dictated that there should be no frills in his cars' design (a fourth wheel being regarded as a frill) and that components should preferably be multi-functional. Thus, for instance, the central chassis member doubled as a torque tube while, in early models, exhaust gases discharged through the lower chassis tubes. This ethos is reprised in the Super 3, particularly in the chassis department. Hot sheet aluminium is vacuum-formed into a central tub to which bulkheads and other substructures are bonded, and stressed body panels are fixed. This assembly is braced at each end with multipurpose aluminium castings. The complex front castings provide, additionally, mounts for the suspension wishbones, steering-rack and engine, and ducting for the twin, side-mounted radiators. They also form the cosmetic 'face' of the car. The rear structure accommodates the lighting, number plate and boot hinge. The car's external 'sideblades' complete the control of airflow through the radiators and act as mounts for bespoke luggage.

From the gearbox rearwards, the drivetrain is similar to the M3W but a three-cylinder, liquid-cooled, 1.5-litre Ford Dragon engine now sits behind the front axle line under the bonnet. This engine does not replicate the harmful torque of the S&S, so a cush-drive is not fitted.

Front suspension is by double wishbones with inboard coil springs operated by levers and pull-rods attached to the outer ends of the upper wishbones. The 20in × 3.5in alloy front wheels are shod with custom-designed Avon tyres and carry 11.5in disc brakes. The wide, 15in × 6in rear alloy with its stock Avon tyre and 9in drum brake sits in a massive, fabricated, coil-sprung fork.

The Super 3 monocoque. (Joris Mans)

# CHAPTER 4

# Morgan Power

It is hard to bring to mind another car that outdoes the magnificently cluttered front end of one of the sportier Morgan three-wheelers. The distinctive bullnose radiator and statuesque overhead-valve V-twin herald the arrival of no ordinary motorcar. The mechanical clamour and exposure of thrashing parts suggest brute power and functionality. Fewer than half of the pre-war cars bore these extrovert characteristics, however (though all Morgans tend to be noisy).

The F-Type, launched in 1933, housed its conventional engine beneath a conventional bonnet and, apart from its lone rear wheel, looked, well, quite conventional. In the preceding twenty-three years – the two-speeder age – by far the most common Morgans were the early Runabouts and the Family model with their austere bodies and engine-shrouding coalscuttle bonnets. They were powered almost exclusively by the 980cc side-valve JAP V-twin, which, although less glamourous than its overhead-valve counterpart, still enabled its lightweight host to outperform most other cars on the road. Matchless engines were to oust JAPs after the 1932/33 transition from two- to three-speeders.

In the early heyday of cyclecars and large-capacity motorcycles, engines of all types and makes were plentiful. HFS and his father ruled out engine manufacture as both unviable and unnecessary in their infant enterprise. It made far better sense to offer customers a choice of proprietary engines bought in from a range of suppliers. This policy still holds firm: Morgan have never built engines. Theoretically it also gave Morgan more flexibility and better bargaining-power, although in truth it was probably JAP's John Prestwich – a far bigger industrial fish than HFS and easily his biggest engine-provider – who held the whip-hand when it came to price negotiations.

A happy design feature of the Morgan two- and three-speeder chassis, for which generations of future owners would be forever thankful, was the remarkable ease with which engines could be swapped. The engine was suspended from the four projecting front chassis tubes by four engine plates sandwiching the engine's crankcase. It was a simple matter to make plates for varying crankcases; the eight outer holes were drilled to slide onto the universally positioned tubes thus ensuring that any engine could fit any Morgan.

All two-speeder engines relied on total loss lubrication. On very early Morgans the driver had to deliver a shot of oil every few minutes by means of a tap and plunger mounted on the bulkhead. The levels of memory and concentration required to accomplish this were somewhat reduced with the advent of the Best and Lloyd pump. Dashboard-mounted, this device needed an observable spring-loaded plunger to be depressed every five to ten minutes. Oil was metered to the engine via an adjustable drip feed until the plunger was fully extended again by its spring, ready for the driver's attention.

Ignition and carburettor control levers were mounted on the steering wheel. Ignition was by magneto, and water-cooling was thermo-syphonic through a tube-and-gill radiator. The later JAP and Matchless engines fitted to three-speeders were similarly cooled but had coil ignition and mechanically pumped dry sump oiling. Air-cooled engines, mainly JAP, were available for some models and, being cheaper and simpler, were a popular option for the Family. A choice of Binks, Brown & Barlow or AMAC carburettor was offered until 1927 when those manufacturers merged to become Amalgamated Carburetters Ltd. Thereafter their 'Amal' products were generally fitted.

Since 1909 Morgan have fitted ten makes of engine to their three-wheeler models in numbers ranging from the lone Peugeot, which powered the prototype Runabout, to over 17,000 assorted JAPs. Although Baker-Precision and Blumfield engines were offered as options early on, it is thought that they were fitted only in tiny numbers.

Controls of a 1921 Morgan showing the Best & Lloyd oil drip-feed on the dashboard, and magneto and carburettor levers mounted left and right on the steering wheel. Wooden pedals, coconut matting, the right-hand gear change and a magneto cut-out switch are also visible. (Author)

# Baker-Precision

During the short life of his company, Frank Baker achieved quite a lot. Founded in Birmingham in 1906, F. E. Baker Ltd developed a range of motorcycle and cyclecar engines under its 'Precision' brand. By 1913 over twenty engines, from 170cc to 964cc, were catalogued and sales – particularly exports – were booming. Baker was a sizeable manufacturer and it is surprising that so few of his engines were fitted to Morgans. The company's fortunes faded after the First World War, and it closed in 1919. Probably fewer than ten of these engines were fitted to Morgans.

**Model:** 8hp
**Type:** 50° V-twin, water-cooled, side-valve
**Bore × stroke and capacity:** 85mm × 85mm, 964cc
**Output:** 20bhp at 2,400rpm (approximately)
**Years offered:** 1912–14
**Applications:** Standard, De Luxe, Sporting, Grand Prix

Precision side-valve, 1914. (C. M. Booth collection)

# Blackburne

Having built motorcycles and engines since 1913, Burney & Blackburn Ltd (confusingly, there was no 'e' in the maker's name) dropped bike-making in 1921 to concentrate on producing proprietary engines from their Atlas Works in Bookham, Surrey. They were soon major suppliers, not just to seventy motorcycle manufacturers but to car and aircraft makers too.

Harry Hatch, the defected chief designer from JAP, created the KM series of water-cooled overhead-valve engines, first fitted to Morgans from 1922 in KMA form. The KMB, an improved, strengthened and tuned version of the KMA, was designed for competition and none were fitted to production cars. The KMC, replacing the KMA, was a detuned version of the KMB. These engines were technically sophisticated, well-engineered and powerful for their day. Moreover, they were designed specifically for cyclecars, having lighter internal flywheels to compensate for the heavy external cone-clutch assemblies they were mated to. Performance of KM-equipped Morgans was, therefore, markedly superior and the Blackburne, despite its considerably higher price, was regarded by many discerning buyers as the engine of choice. No overhead-valve JAP was available in a Morgan between 1922 and 1925 so options during that period were restricted to the Blackburne and the cheaper but lower-powered Anzani. Admirable air- and water-cooled side-valve models VCM and ZCM, based on the KM bottom end, were also available between 1922 and 1924 and fitted in small numbers.

About 540 Blackburnes, of all types, were fitted to Morgans.

Blackburne VCM side-valve, 1922. (Author)

Blackburne KM overhead-valve, 1924. (Author)

**Model:** KMA and KMC
**Type:** 60° V-twin, water-cooled, overhead-valve
**Bore × stroke and capacity:** 85mm × 96.8mm, 1,098cc
**Output:** 35bhp at 4,000rpm (KMA); 40bhp at 4,000 (KMC)
**Years offered:** 1922–26 (KMA); 1926–27 (KMC)
**Applications:** Grand Prix (KMA only), Aero, Aero Family

# Blumfield

Blumfield Ltd had some success in building motorcycles and engines but enjoyed an even shorter productive life than F. E. Baker Ltd. Founded in 1910 by T. W. Blumfield, it offered a narrower range of motorcycle and cyclecar engines until 1914 when manufacturing activities ceased permanently. Smaller manufacturers struggled to compete against both the pricing and fine reputation of JAP at this time.

Probably fewer than ten Blumfield engines were fitted to Morgans.

**Model:** 8/10hp
**Type:** 50° V-twin, air or water-cooled, side-valve
**Bore × stroke and capacity:** 81.5mm × 95mm, 991cc
**Output:** 20bhp at 2,000rpm
**Years offered:** 1912–14
**Applications:** Standard, De Luxe, Sporting, Grand Prix

# British Anzani

The Italian Alessandro Anzani operated from headquarters in Paris. He founded his reputation as an engine designer and manufacturer on Louis Blériot's successful first flight across the Channel aboard his Anzani-powered flying-machine in 1909. The British Anzani Engine Company Ltd was established in London in 1912, initially to manufacture Anzani aero-engines under licence for the British market. Despite a somewhat chaotic business style, much of its life being spent in receivership, the company managed to produce well-designed engines – if of sometimes questionable quality.

Anzani CCW overhead-valve cyclecar engines were first available in Morgans in 1923. Blackburne was their sole competitor for Morgan's overhead-valve market until 1925 when the JAP LTOW appeared. The Anzani was the cheapest of the overhead-valve engine options. Poor quality exhaust valves resulted in multiple engine failures and consequent guarantee claims against Morgan. HFS's cancellation of his current order, and subsequent legal action, contributed to Anzani's bankruptcy in 1927. Unbowed, the company reformed and operated under the auspices of Archie Frazer Nash Ltd, an existing customer for its four-cylinder engines. All was forgiven, it seems, as Morgan soon resumed buying the restyled M3 engine – much the same as the CCW but with heads and valve-gear revised to eliminate the earlier flaws.

About 880 Anzani engines were fitted to Morgans.

**Model:** CCW and M3
**Type:** 57° V-twin, water-cooled, overhead-valve
**Bore × stroke and capacity:** 85mm × 95mm, 1,078cc
**Output:** 26bhp at 3,000rpm
**Years offered:** 1923–25 (CCW); 1926–31 (M3)
**Applications:** Grand Prix (CCW only), Aero, Family, De Luxe

Anzani M3
overhead-valve,
1927. (Author)

# Ford

There is something so British about the little 1930s Model Y Ford 8 that it is easy to overlook its American ancestry. Though built in Dagenham, the only fully equipped saloon car ever to sell for £100 was designed entirely in the USA. It first appeared in late 1932 and as HFS was testing engines for his all-new three-wheeler at about the same time, he must have concluded that the Ford 8hp side-valve engine would be not only eminently suitable but also reliable and cheap. F-type Morgans were equipped wholly satisfactorily with this or the 10hp Model C version until production ceased in 1952.

All the 830 F-type Morgans built were fitted with Ford 8hp or 10hp engines.

**Model:** Y (E04A) 8hp and C (E93A) 10hp
**Type:** in-line four cylinder, water-cooled, side-valve
**Bore × stroke and capacity:** 56.6mm × 92.5mm, 933cc (8hp); 63.5mm × 92.5mm, 1,172cc (10hp)
**Output:** 23bhp at 4,000rpm (8hp); 30bhp at 4,000rpm
**Years offered:** 1934–46 (8hp); 1936–52 (10hp)
**Applications:** F4, F2, F Super (10hp only)

Ford introduced their three-cylinder Ecoboost Dragon engine in 2014. Morgan chose it for the Morgan Super 3 for its light weight and compact proportions which allow it to be mounted behind the front axle line of the car for optimum weight distribution. Sensibly,

Ford C 10hp side-valve, 1936. (Author)

Ford Dragon engine sitting in the Super 3's multipurpose castings. (Joris Mans)

the turbocharger is removed to reduce power output from around 200bhp to 118bhp. The facility for running on only two cylinders to optimise fuel consumption is probably not a feature that Super 3 owners will hurry to activate.

**Model:** Dragon
**Type:** in-line three cylinder, liquid-cooled, twin overhead-camshaft
**Bore × stroke and capacity:** 79mm × 76.4mm, 1.5 litre
**Output:** 118bhp at 6,500rpm
**Years offered:** 2022–
**Application:** Super 3

## JAP

The early histories of Morgan and JAP are inseparable. John Alfred Prestwich was an engineering genius, inventor and entrepreneur who became Britain's biggest proprietary motorcycle engine manufacturer between the wars. Born in 1874, the son of a photographer, Prestwich had developed an exceptional flair for designing and building machines, particularly engines, by the age of fourteen. In 1894, having served an engineering apprenticeship, he formed the Prestwich Manufacturing Co. to make and sell scientific instruments from a small workshop at the family home in Tottenham, North London. He married in 1896 and set up his first home, with an adjacent small factory, still in Tottenham.

No doubt influenced by his father's profession, he was attracted to the emerging motion picture industry and soon established himself as a leading inventor and manufacturer of movie cameras and projection equipment.

From time to time over the next few years, however, Prestwich revisited his first love, the internal combustion engine. In 1902 he designed and manufactured a 293cc clip-on motorcycle engine which sold well and was quickly followed by a complete range. In 1911, after a period of immense hard work and innovation, Prestwich acquired Northumberland Park, Tottenham, an industrial site which, over the next decades, he developed from modest beginnings to a vast and advanced manufacturing complex employing a workforce of over 2,000. His passions for best engineering practice and rigorous quality control, and the unrivalled success of his engines in competition, had sealed the reputation of the JAP marque and yielded great commercial rewards. J. A. Prestwich & Co. Ltd despatched its millionth engine from Northumberland Park in 1948 and was well on the way to its second million, by then mostly small industrial models, when it merged with Villiers in 1957. A few years later the conglomerate fell victim to the advancing Japanese motorcycle industry and closed.

JAP announced its 8hp side-valve V-twin in 1909 and versions of the KT and KTW were fitted in large numbers to certain Morgans continuously from 1910 to 1935. The legendary 90-Bore 90mm x 85mm overhead-valve engine was offered by Morgan from 1912 to 1920 but was rarely fitted. Good-looking and powerful, it was also fragile and unreliable and sold only in limited numbers. Today, despite its shortcomings, it represents the holy grail for JAP enthusiasts.

Holy grail. JAP '90-Bore' overhead-valve, 1914. (Sue Clark)

A long pause after the withdrawal of the 90-Bore ended with the arrival in 1925 of the LTOW, the first of the 50° LT series of potent water-cooled overhead-valve engines that would power the sporting two-speeder Morgans until 1931. The launch that year of the LTOWZ, a 60° up-rated version of the LTOW, was timed to coincide with the arrival of the new three-speeder chassis. Equivalent air- and water-cooled side-valve engines were also announced.

JAP preferred to tweak existing designs rather than initiate new ones and by this time their venerable engines were becoming outdated. This, and perennial pricing disputes with Prestwich, had prompted HFS to seek an alternative supplier and in 1933 Matchless Motorcycles (Colliers) Ltd stepped in with a new, modern range. JAP engines were available for the next two years – presumably to run down stocks – and the last JAP-powered car left the factory in February 1936.

Approximately 17,400 JAP engines were fitted to Morgans. A representative, but not exhaustive, selection of JAP specifications follows:

**Model:** 8hp and 'Small Port' KT and KTW
**Type:** 50° V-twin, air or water-cooled, side-valve
**Bore × stroke and capacity:** 85mm × 85mm, 964cc, then 85.7mm × 85mm, 980cc
**Output:** 20bhp (approximately) at 2,300rpm
**Years offered:** 1910–25
**Applications:** Standard, De Luxe, Sporting, Grand Prix, Family, Aero

JAP 8hp side-valve, 1914. These 'Small Port' engines and their later KT (air-cooled) and KTW (water-cooled) derivatives powered the majority of Morgans. (Author)

**Model:** 'Big Port' KT and KTW
**Type:** 50° V-twin, air or water-cooled, side-valve
**Bore × stroke and capacity:** 85.7mm × 85mm, 980cc
**Output:** 25bhp at 2,600rpm (a/c), 26bhp at 2,600rpm (w/c)
**Years offered:** 1921–32
**Applications:** Standard, De Luxe, Grand Prix, Family, Aero, Delivery Van

**Model:** LTOW
**Type:** 50° V-twin, water-cooled, overhead-valve
**Bore × stroke and capacity:** 85.7mm × 95mm, 1,098cc
**Output:** 40bhp at 4,200rpm
**Years offered:** 1925–32
**Applications:** Aero, Super Sports Aero, Aero Family

**Model:** LTOWZ
**Type:** 60° V-twin, water-cooled, overhead-valve
**Bore × stroke and capacity:** 85.7mm × 95mm, 1,098cc
**Output:** 39bhp at 4,500rpm
**Years offered:** 1932–35
**Applications:** Super Sports, Sports 2-Seater, Sports Family

JAP 'Big Port' KTW side-valve, 1929. Note the Morgan engine plates. (Author)

JAP LTOW 'Dogear'
overhead-valve, 1929.
(Author)

JAP LTOWZ overhead-valve, fitted to some three-speeders from 1932 to 1935. (Author)

# MAG (Motosacoche, Acacias, Geneva)

The Swiss manufacturer launched its cyclecar engine in 1914. Despite its odd appearance and valve-arrangement, it was a well-engineered and reasonably powerful and reliable engine. It was outdated by 1924 when, following failure to agree prices with MAG, HFS removed it from the Morgan catalogue.

Around 420 MAG engines were fitted to Morgans.

**Model:** 2C13A (air-cooled) and 2C20A (water-cooled)
**Type:** 45° V-twin, air- or water-cooled, inlet-over-exhaust valves
**Bore × stroke and capacity:** 82mm × 104mm, 1,094cc
**Output:** 26bhp at 2,600rpm
**Years offered:** 1914–24
**Applications:** Grand Prix, Sporting, De Luxe

MAG 2C20A overhead inlet-valve, side-valve exhaust, 1922. (C. M. Booth collection)

# Matchless

Henry Herbert Collier founded his Matchless bicycle-building business in the 1890s in Plumstead, South-East London. His sons Charlie and Harry joined him soon afterwards and Matchless motorcycles were produced from 1901, initially powered by proprietary engines, often of JAP manufacture. Matchless built their own engines from 1912 and their first V-twin, a 990cc side-valve, was launched in 1925. This was subsequently styled the Model X and was to be the basis of the three engine types specifically designed for the Morgan in 1933 – the MX (water-cooled, side-valve), MX2 (air-cooled, overhead-valve) and MX4 (water-cooled, overhead-valve) of which 654, 224 and 388, respectively, were fitted to Morgans. These powerful engines were solidly built, reliable, quiet (relative to JAPs) and smooth-running.

**Model:** MX
**Type:** 50° V-twin, water-cooled, side-valve
**Bore × stroke and capacity:** 85.5mm × 85.5mm, 990cc
**Output:** 27.5bhp at 4,000rpm
**Years offered:** 1933–37
**Applications:** Sports 2-Seater, Family, Delivery Van

Matchless MX side-valve, 1935. The optional, faux-finned alloy covers protected the plugs and added style. (C. M. Booth collection)

Matchless MX2 overhead-valve, 1936. (Author)


**Model:** MX2 (air-cooled) and MX4 (water-cooled)
**Type:** 50° V-twin, air or water-cooled, overhead-valve
**Bore × stroke and capacity:** 85.5mm × 85.5mm, 990cc
**Output:** 39.1bhp at 4,600rpm (a/c), 42bhp at 4,800rpm (w/c)
**Years offered:** 1933–38 (MX2), 1934–39 (MX4)
**Applications:** Super Sports, Sports 2-Seater, Sports Family


## Peugeot

Even as HFS fitted a redundant 7hp Peugeot engine to his prototype monocar it is likely that his thoughts were turning to the JAP range for future production models. The Peugeot's dated automatic inlet arrangement, whereby the engine's suction on the inlet stroke opened the valve against a weak spring, was a hit-and-miss affair which would always compromise power output and engine speed. JAP engines with their fully mechanical valve-gear were, indeed, soon adopted.

**Model:** Y 8hp
**Type:** 45° V-twin, air-cooled, side-valve (automatic inlet, mechanical exhaust)
**Bore × stroke and capacity:** 75mm × 75mm, 633cc
**Output:** 12bhp at 1,500rpm (approximately)
**Application:** Fitted to 1909 prototype only

Peugeot Frères side-valve engine as fitted by H. F. S. Morgan to his prototype in 1909. (Author)

## S&S

S&S Cycle of Viola, Wisconsin, have been building motorcycle engines since the 1950s and are now second only in size to Harley-Davidson as engine manufacturers in the USA. They launched their X-Wedge V-twin in 2007 as an H-D replacement engine and it was fitted to the M3W throughout production from 2012 to 2021. It was very much in the tradition of the Morgan three-wheeler, although, being nearly twice the size of the largest pre-war engine fitted, its thumping performance was rather more startling. It boasted all mod cons, including fuel injection, catalytic converter and a toothed timing belt. Owners were relieved to learn that the inevitable failure of said belt would result merely in a bus ride home and a new belt rather than a replacement engine. Early on it was discovered that the engine produced huge spikes of torque during its firing cycle – way beyond its quoted maximum output – which, untamed, caused rapid destruction of gearboxes. This unwelcome characteristic was suppressed by the insertion of a cush-drive between engine and gearbox. The X-Wedge failed stricter US emissions testing in 2020 when S&S ceased its manufacture, thus prompting the M3W's demise.

All the 2,500 (approximately) M3W Morgans were fitted with S&S X-Wedge engines.

**Model:** X-Wedge
**Type:** 56° V-twin, air-cooled, overhead-valve
**Bore × stroke and capacity:** 107.95mm × 107.95mm, 1,976cc
**Output:** 82bhp at 5,250rpm
**Years offered:** 2012–21
**Application:** M3W

S&S Wedge overhead-valve. (Author)

# CHAPTER 5

# Morgan Two-Speeders

HFS's two-speeder chassis had a simple but ingenious transmission system. The two wide-spaced gear ratios worked well for a cyclecar propelled by a relatively powerful engine. The absence of a reverse gear was a trifle inconvenient but the cars were light and could be easily manhandled by a dismounted driver or passenger. Solo drivers soon learned to make use of banks and inclines to reverse while remaining *in situ*. The earliest of these diminutive runabouts had a 6ft wheelbase, lengthened after the First World War to 6ft 11in. Track measurements varied between 4ft and 4ft 2in. For their time Morgans were inexpensive and reliable and offered surprisingly exciting performance.

Chassis and transmission were continuously developed, improved and strengthened over a twenty-year life to cope with the ever-increasing power, weight and speed of new models, but by the end of the 1920s few car buyers would tolerate the need to get out and push, let alone the other privations of Morgan ownership; well aware of what Austin, Morris and others had to offer they were, by now, far too sophisticated for all that. In 1931 the two-speeders had to make way for the next generation, though a few more were sold to special order and at clearance prices, the last ever, an unusual Anzani-powered Super Aero, leaving Pickersleigh Road on 23 May 1933. The 18,229 two-speeders built represented 86 per cent of all Morgan three-wheeler output up to 1952.

A word on Morgan dates: this applies to all three-wheelers built between 1910 and 1952. The 'model year' ran from 1 October to the following 30 September and the latest range of models was announced at November's London Olympia Motor Cycle Show. So, for example, the 1929 models were launched at the November 1928 show and manufactured between October 1928 and September 1929. Strictly, a car is dated by the year of its registration, which tends to correspond with the model year and the year of manufacture – but not always. For instance, a 1929 model built in October 1928 would probably have been sold and registered in 1928 and would therefore have been a 1928 car.

# Standard, De Luxe and Sporting – 1911 to 1931

Who said 'badge engineering' was a mid-century thing? HFS himself might well have devised it forty years earlier to market the first three cars in his 1911–14 ranges. There was little to differentiate the Standard (think Mini-Minor), De Luxe (Mini-Minor Super) and Sporting (Riley Elf) models other than slight body variations and thickness of upholstery (though the 1913 Grand Prix (Mini Cooper) was genuinely superior). But it made good business sense to offer an apparent range of cars to suit variations in taste and depth of pocket.

Before the First World War these three models had a 6ft wheelbase and were powered by air-cooled, side-valve 8hp JAP engines. Transmission gave two forward speeds and no reverse. There was a choice of grey or green paint, with embellishment to taste, and windscreen, hood and lighting sets were fitted only at extra cost. The steering was not geared, and the hand and foot brakes comprised lined, sprung steel bands contracting onto separate drums on either side of the rear wheel. Top speed was 45mph, cruising speed 35mph and fuel consumption 60mpg. Weight was just 3cwt. Tyres were 26in × 2½in beaded-edge.

The early Standard, the cheapest model, had austere bodywork with open sides and exposed rear wheel. It was dropped from the range after 1914 but reintroduced for the 1922 season as the Standard Popular, retaining the 8hp air-cooled JAP and, uniquely, the 6ft wheelbase. It now shared the styling of the De Luxe and Family models but sported a boat tail. Windscreen, hood and lighting were included in the £150 price. The model was discontinued in 1928. Built in their thousands, only a dozen or so have survived.

The De Luxe had elbow-height body sides, mudguards for all three wheels and a passenger-side door. Comfort was considerably enhanced by a thickly upholstered, sprung seat-squab and seat-back. Post-war, the longer wheelbase Grand Prix chassis was specified and the option of a water-cooled 8hp JAP added. Essentials such as windscreen, hood and lighting were now fitted as standard equipment. The body style looked dated by 1921 and the flat sides and rounded tail of the Family model were adopted from 1922. The De Luxe ceased production in 1931.

Standard runabout
from the 1913
catalogue.
(Morgan Motor Co.)

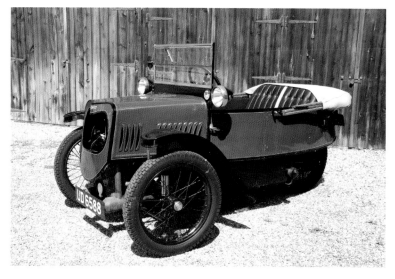

The Standard
model's short
wheelbase, tiny
door and cute
boat tail give it
a charm all of
its own. This is
a 1927 example.
(Author)

De Luxe runabout
from the 1913
catalogue.
(Morgan
Motor Co.)

De Luxe model
from the 1929
catalogue.
(Morgan
Motor Co.)

The early Sporting was, in truth, no more 'sporting' than its stablemates. Its doorless body and narrow tail were sporty in their way, but once the Grand Prix arrived the car seemed to have little point. The post-war version was built on the longer chassis of the Grand Prix but retained its coalscuttle bonnet and air-cooled engine. It was permanently dropped in 1921.

Sporting runabout from the 1913 catalogue. (Morgan Motor Co.)

1913 Sporting runabout. (Author)

# Grand Prix – 1913 to 1926

Despite being spirited and dependable performers on- and off-road, the first Morgans presented a rather old-fashioned, utilitarian image. Even the Sporting model had a distinctly Edwardian look.

Early in 1913 HFS started work on a new model which, with improved handling, racier lines and a new overhead-valve water-cooled JAP engine, would appeal to those of his clientele with sporting aspirations. At this time l'Automobile Club de France announced that its first French Cyclecar Grand Prix would be staged on the forthcoming 13 July at Amiens. Conscious that an appearance at Amiens would, if successful, make a dazzling launch opportunity for the new model, HFS pulled out all stops to complete a prototype for testing in the London–Edinburgh Trial in May, though the new 90-Bore JAP became available only shortly before the French race. Of the three Morgan starters at Amiens, only one finished – but that was enough. It stormed to victory in the hands of W. G. McMinnies and HFS immediately and triumphantly unveiled the new 'Grand Prix' model.

The wheelbase of the Grand Prix was, at 6ft 11in, 11 inches longer than standard. This was to enable the seats to be mounted on the floor in front of the bevel box rather than above it, thus considerably lowering the car's centre of gravity. The track was wider and the chassis tubes were increased from 1in to 1¼in diameter to increase stiffness. Water-cooled engines were always fitted; despite their added weight and complexity they ran more reliably at sustained high speeds. The engine sat, exposed, in front of a handsome bullnose radiator, setting the familiar Morgan style that endured until 1939. The body was sleek, modern and rakish.

Three versions of the car were initially listed: the No. 1, with a narrow, sporting body and side-valve JAP; the No. 2 with a wider, touring body and side-valve JAP and the No. 3 – a replica of the race-winning car, complete with 90-Bore JAP and capable of 65mph. The Grand Prix was an instant hit in Britain and France and became Morgan's flagship model for some years.

Father and daughter sally forth in 1915. All Grand Prix were water-cooled; this one is fitted with a side-valve JAP. (Author's collection)

A 1914 Grand Prix model confronts its nemesis, an Austin Seven, outside a Bristol pub in the mid-1920s. The engine is a JAP 90-Bore. (Martyn Webb collection)

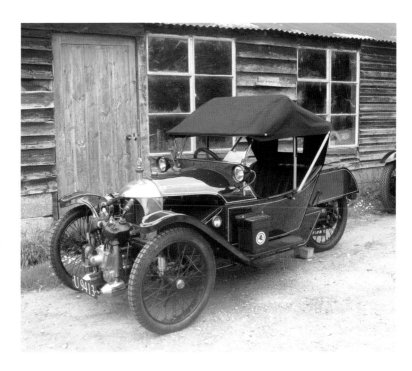

Most Grand Prix were powered by the JAP KTW – here the small port version. The hood keeps off the evening dew, but little else. (Sue Clark)

The car evolved gently in its thirteen-year life. The styling altered subtly, taking its final raffish form from around 1920. Only MAG engines were offered on the handful of cars built during the First World War. The side-valve JAP was always the favourite, but MAG and overhead-valve Anzani and Blackburne engines were also available in the 1920s. Front-wheel brakes were an optional extra from 1923.

The Grand Prix was finally dropped from the catalogue in 1926, by which time it had been fully supplanted by the Aero.

# Aero – 1920 to 1932

Legend has it that, in the infancy of a new model, HFS would draw a life-size profile of the car he envisaged on the factory wall and delegate the body-shop foreman to experiment in wood and metal until a satisfactory three-dimensional interpretation had been produced. On the day he chalked up the Aero, his creative juices must have been in full flow as, of all the three-wheelers, this was perhaps the most pleasing on the eye, its graceful fuselage, pretty wings and disc wheels offering Biggles fantasists the next best thing to a Sopwith Camel.

It has been suggested that the 'mystery' model which first appeared in 1916 and was later linked with air ace Captain Albert Ball VC DSO MC and his chums, was the first Aero prototype. This seems unlikely, though, so soon after the introduction of the Grand Prix in 1913. The MAG-engined car had a long, streamlined tail and staggered seats, but was in all other respects a Grand Prix. It did not have a model name but could be bought to special order. Nevertheless, by the end of the decade HFS had a new, ultra-sporting model in mind.

Although the Aero was officially announced and named at the 1919 Olympia Show it was only available to special order and in limited numbers for the 1920 to 1923 seasons. By 1922 the car still had the air of a Grand Prix with a longer, wider tail grafted on. A competition version powered by an eight-valve overhead-camshaft Anzani engine had been making its mark at Brooklands that year and it was this car – the 'Flat-Sided' or '200-Mile' Aero with its clean, seamless shape – that set the style for the production car that was unveiled at the 1923 show and finally entered the 1924 catalogue.

The exposed engine and bullnose radiator were retained. The bonnet sides were now enclosed by hinged, louvred panels. Flat section wings curved over the front wheels, then dived gracefully down and back to a delicate point. The one-piece side body panels flowed, pleasingly uninterrupted, from scuttle to upswept stern, arching up to form a horizontal platform behind the cockpit and terminating in a delicious little compound-curve tail.

This 1924 Aero was upgraded to Blackburne power. Further extras include 'ship's ventilator' air ducts to the footwell, central searchlight (for big game?) and wheel discs... (Author)

All this was topped off with aero-screens, miniature ship's ventilators and a snake's head bulb-horn. Although the Aero was primarily designed as a high performer, the worthy side-valve JAP was offered alongside the more exotic overhead-valve Blackburne, Anzani and JAP engines throughout the life of the model and it was a popular, cheaper, option. The higher-powered engines provided 70mph performance.

The flowing wings fitted to the 1924 cars were replaced in 1925 with the distinctive 'elephant-ear' type. Enhancements such as front-wheel brakes, the wider, stronger bevel box, a self-starter and steering reduction-gear became available as the development of the two-speeder chassis progressed. In common with the rest of the range the Aero and, for 1931 only, the Aero De Luxe, could be built on the under-slung M-Type chassis from 1930. Heavily discounted two-speeder Aeros continued to be sold in very limited numbers and a rare edition of thirty-five three-speeders was built before the last of the line left the factory in December 1932.

It is thought that of the approximately 2,300 Aeros built, 189 (8 per cent) have survived.

...It is fitted with the flowing wings characteristic of early Aeros. (Author)

Fairest of them all? The Aero from the 1929 catalogue with distinctive 'elephant-ear' wings. (Morgan Motor Co.)

# Family – 1922 to 1933

Like the Beast of Bodmin Moor, sightings of the four-seater Family model were rare and fleeting – and only in prototype form – before it finally emerged from the shadows and went on sale in 1922. HFS had begun designs for this car ten years earlier, but the war and factory capacity issues had led to several false starts. It was a daring launch: the Austin Seven offensive had begun and affection for the cyclecar was evaporating. Nevertheless, of all their three-wheelers, the Family was to become Morgan's best seller.

The car was initially built on the now regular 6ft 11in Narrow B chassis and then the Wide B from 1926 when front-wheel brakes became standard. A De Luxe version on the M-Type chassis was offered for the 1931 season. The body was of similar style to the contemporary two-seater De Luxe: flat-sided, round-tailed and perpendicular, it had simple lines and was not unappealing. Access to the rear seats was through a door on the passenger side, facilitated by a folding front seat which was also adjustable to provide a few inches of rear

Two-speeder Family from the 1929 catalogue. The starting-handle socket just forward of the rear tyre, and the decompressor lever mounted on the bodywork above it are typical of all two-speeders. (Morgan Motor Co.)

Mum, Dad and the boys enjoy a rural outing in a two-speeder Family in August 1929. Mum is behind the Box Brownie. (Author's collection)

legroom. Three small children could be accommodated aft, but there was really insufficient legroom for adults. A folding hood was included but side screens were extra. A side-valve JAP, generally air-cooled, propelled the car at 50mpg to cruising and top speeds of 45mph and 50mph respectively. Alternatively, an overhead-valve Anzani or side-valve Blackburne could be specified. The two-speeder Family was still available to special order in 1933, by which time the three-speeder version had all but superseded it.

These cars are now very rare; only forty of the estimated 7,200 built are known to have survived. Most were driven into the ground or converted into more supposedly desirable models.

## Delivery Van – 1914 and 1928 to 1931

The Morgan chassis, though perfect for its intended use, was ill-suited as the platform for a van. The intrusion of the boxed-in rear wheel and suspension into the load-carrying area confined much of the 3cwt payload to the upper area of the van body, placing considerable strain on the wheel and springs and compromising the vehicle's centre of gravity and stability. Van-buyers were quick to identify these flaws and, by and large, gave the Delivery Van a wide berth.

Convertible bodywork was a popular idea in Edwardian motoring. For 1914 only, HFS introduced the Commercial Carrier, a simple, wooden pickup body which could be bolted onto the rear of the Standard model as and when required. Carrying capacity was restricted to 1¾cwt and only a handful were sold. In 1928, with similar lack of success, he launched the larger, covered Convertible Carrier, compatible with the Family body. Next year, ever optimistic, he followed this with a purpose-built, 3cwt-payload Delivery Van built on the short, Standard model chassis. It kept the JAP KT engine, bonnet, wings and side door of the Standard while a curved roof swept back from the windscreen top over flat, upright sides to double doors at the back. It remained in the two-speeder catalogue until 1931.

The 1929 3cwt Delivery Van. Lovable, but top heavy. (Morgan Motor Co.)

'Your comestibles Madam'. Late 1920s sketch. (Morgan Motor Co.)

Quaint and charming though it now seems, the two-speeder Delivery Van was never well regarded. In the four years it was listed, only twenty-one were sold, none of which have survived. The model did, however, live on – just as unsuccessfully – for a further four years in three-speeder form.

## Aero Family – 1927 to 1930; Sports Family – 1931

Demand for a sporting four-seater was sparse in the two-speeder era, though, later, the cars sold a little better in three-speeder form.

The Aero Family was never listed in the Morgan catalogue. It was the brainchild of the London Morgan agent Arthur Maskell for whom the first car was built to special order in 1926. A rear body with seats and curved tail, à la Family, replaced the upswept rear of an otherwise standard Blackburne-engined Aero. It was then available to special order in this guise until 1930, fitted with the Blackburne for 1927 and the LTOW JAP thereafter. These Morgans are very rare birds; of the estimated fifteen built, only two genuine examples survive.

The two-speeder Sports Family was a listed model for 1931 only. The body was similar to the Aero Family but boat-tailed and mounted on the C-type chassis in preparation for the transition to the three-speed range in 1932. Although the LTOW was standard equipment, a side-valve JAP could also be specified. As rare as its predecessor, only twenty-one two-speed examples were built; four survive.

For one year only. The rare 1931 two-speeder Sports Family. (Arnold Marshall)

## Super Sports Aero – 1928 to 1931

'A very demon on wheels' was Morgan's own description of the Super Sports Aero in its 1927 launch publicity for Olympia. Yet again HFS had conceived a showstopper. It was the fastest and lowest-slung production Morgan ever built and defined the look and character of the sporting models for the next eleven years. Although there was little mechanically to differentiate the Super Sports Aero from the Aero, the new car's styling and lower stance marked the transition from roaring 1920s grace to 1930s streamline moderne.

The 1928 and 1929 'Super Aeros', as they came to be known, were built on the Wide B chassis with its top front cross-tube cranked upwards, lower lugs inverted and rear springs underslung to reduce height by 2½in below the standard Aero. Initially, two Hartford rear shock absorbers were fitted, Newtons being added to the front a year later. From 1930 the new, superior M-Type chassis, now with both front cross-tubes cranked, was offered; it was specified by nearly all customers.

The overhead-valve JAP sat, al fresco as ever, forward of the signature bullnose radiator and one-piece bonnet and scuttle. The squat, streamlined torpedo body terminated beyond the cockpit in a beetleback with a hinged top giving access to the rear wheel and chains. Simple, fixed cycle mudguards were later replaced by the valanced type. The passenger seat was staggered slightly aft to allow the driver more elbowroom within the narrower body. The scuttle, beneath tiny aero-screens, extended rearwards a few inches on the passenger side. The oil filler sat behind a cut-out in the bonnet on the driver's side and the gear-change lever was mounted outside the cockpit. Super Aeros were all powered by the JAP LTOW '10/40' engine, specially tuned with high compression heads and a twin-float sports carburettor giving a claimed performance of 80mph. Overall, the car had a very sporting and rather pugnacious look. 'Demon on wheels' was no overstatement.

This model was to remain the fastest of the three-wheelers until the advent of the five-speeders and is regarded by many connoisseurs as the most desirable of them all.

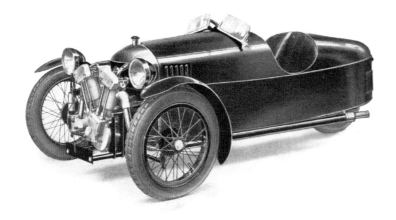

'A very demon on wheels'. Super Sports Aero from the 1929 catalogue. (Morgan Motor Co.)

Dream machine. The only factory-built, Blackburne-engined Super Sports Aero – considered by some buffs to be the perfect Morgan marriage. Built in 1929 and photographed with its owner, Reginald Baker, in 1931. (Christian Baker collection)

A 1930 Super Aero sprinting in 2007. (Grahame Joseph collection)

Renamed Super Sports for 1931 – its last year of production as a two-speeder – it transitioned almost seamlessly into the three-speeder Super Sports of 1932. Around 550 were built, of which an impressive 166 (30 per cent) remain.

## The French Darmont Morgans

The French may have howled with indignation at McMinnies' thrashing of their countryman Henri Bourbeau's Bédélia – a thoroughly inferior and outdated car – in the 1913 Cyclecar Grand Prix, but in the aftermath they wanted to buy Morgans with a passion. That passion was frustrated by the First World War but was reignited in 1919 when sales of the De Luxe and Grand Prix models to France were re-established. However, the heavy import duty on vehicles threatened to stifle any further sales growth, so in 1922 HFS granted a licence to Paris agents Darmont et Badelogue to manufacture 'Darmont-Morgans'. The marque would continue to flourish in France and HFS, with very little effort, would earn a royalty for every car built. As this arrangement progressed, the French content of the cars grew until, by 1925, Darmont were even manufacturing JAP and Blackburne engines under their own name.

The first models, the Sporting and the Sport, were based respectively on the De Luxe and Grand Prix Morgans. Darmont made their own improvements: a reinforced chassis, front shock absorbers, an easily detachable rear wheel and automatic engine-oiling. The Sporting model closely resembled the De Luxe. Its 8hp JAP took it to 50mph. Front wheel brakes were not fitted.

The sleek Sport model had a long, domed tail, a narrower bonnet and radiator than the Grand Prix and skinny, sweeping flat-section mudguards. The engine choices were the air- or water-cooled 8hp JAP or the inlet-over-exhaust MAG which could propel it to 63mph.

In 1923 the 8hp JAP-engined Camionnette was added to the range. Essentially a Sporting with a primitive wooden pickup body mounted over the rear wheel, it was intended for *boulangers* and *épiciers*. Very French.

The Darmont Spécial was introduced in 1927. Aimed at the sportsman, it was very fast and hugely stylish. The long bonnet swept back from a narrow radiator past an oversized steering wheel to an elongated tail reminiscent of the sporting Amilcars and Salmsons. At first there were no mudguards, but front-wheel brakes were standard equipment. Darmont's own version of the Blackburne KMC engine, with twin magnetos and two plugs per head, propelled the Spécial to 93mph. These cars are very rare and are revered by three-wheeler enthusiasts on both sides of the Channel.

Darmont discontinued production of three-wheelers in 1936 and did not survive beyond 1939 after a brief flirtation with four-wheeled cars.

Darmont Spécial, 1928. Observe Darmont's version of the Blackburne KMC engine, exquisite Marchal headlamps and the unique occasional third 'seat'... (Alain Wilczynski)

...Very French! (Alain Wilczynski)

# CHAPTER 6

# Morgan Three-Speeders

By 1930 annual two-speeder sales had halved to fewer than 800 cars in the space of two years. If Morgan was to hold its own among the modern, often mass-produced, competition there was some urgent updating to be done. The rituals of push-reversing, hand-cranking and mending inner tubes at the roadside were really no longer acceptable.

The new, 1932-season three-speeder models were launched at the 1931 Olympia Show, but their characters were not fully formed until a year later when, not before time, they acquired detachable wheels – a refinement that the Austin Seven, among others, had been boasting for ten years. For that interim 1932 year, however, a spare wheel did not have to be accommodated, and bodies kept their familiar svelte form. The Burman three-speed and reverse gearbox was a major advance but did not allow for side-cranking, so the new range of 60° JAPs made provision for a front starting handle. Three-speeders also had the benefit of self-starters. Over the next two years JAPs were phased out in favour of Matchless engines. All three-speeders had a wheelbase of 7ft 3in and a 4ft 2in track.

Dunlop Magna detachable and interchangeable wheels were all very well but, for them to fulfil their purpose, space had to be found for a spare, so 1933 bodies were restyled and strengthened to carry one on the tail. The 1933 facelifts for some older models, notably the Family and the Sports Family, were not altogether successful visually, though the Sports and Super Sports escaped with their good looks. However, with the combined weights of a spare, a gearbox and bulkier bodywork, corpulence threatened: by 1935 a Super Sports weighed 8½cwt – well over the limit for lower road tax, a full 1 hundredweight heavier than a 1929 Super Aero and over twice the weight of a 1921 Grand Prix.

## Delivery Van – 1932 to 1935

The introductory 1932 van was built on the standard-length three-speeder chassis. The front end of the Family model was mated to a curved-roof body reminiscent of the two-speeder van. From 1933 a roomier, flat-roofed body was specified. All three-speeder vans had a 4cwt maximum payload. The air- or water-cooled side-valve 60° JAPs specified for 1932 were thereafter phased out in favour of Matchless MX engines.

Nine vans were built in 1932 and a further twenty-three in the following three years. None have survived but two replicas exist and an original van chassis is known to be flourishing beneath Super Sports bodywork. HFS finally conceded defeat and withdrew the model in 1935.

## Sports Family – 1932 to 1936

Morgan buyers continued to be slow to appreciate the attractions of a sporting four-seater combining rear accommodation and elegant coachwork with potent JAP 10/40 performance. It was the perfect touring Morgan but somehow never caught on.

For 1932 the first three-speeder versions were built on R-type chassis. The body was similar to its two-speeder counterpart but had a curved rather than a boat tail. The 60° side-valve LTWZ JAP could be specified as an alternative to the 10/40. This was a good-looking and powerful model, of which twenty-one were built. It is now greatly admired.

A further ninety-three revised cars left the factory in the following four years. Built on the D-type chassis, these came with detachable Dunlop Magna wheels, a square then barrel-back tail with spare wheel, doors and a wide choice of JAP and Matchless engines. The pairing of the pretty front end of the Sports with the ungainly derrière of the Family was, however, not a happy one aesthetically. About half have, apparently, survived.

The model was dropped, together with the Family, in 1936 after which the F4 remained as the only three-wheeled four-seater.

## Family – 1932 to 1936

Naturally, having been Morgan's best seller for so long, the Family was included in the new three-speeder range. To capitalise on the model's popularity, it was also available to die-hards in two-speeder form until 1933 at reduced price. A lidded luggage-locker supplanted the rear seats in a novel two-seater version catalogued for 1932 and 1933; there is no evidence that any were sold.

New styling coincided with the arrival of Dunlop Magnas for 1933. The rounded bonnet and cowl, valanced cycle-wings and forward-mounted headlamps presented a less Edwardian image. At a pinch, the more spacious cabin could accommodate four adults, behind whom the body terminated in a flat, sloping panel for mounting the spare wheel – upgraded to barrelback styling from 1934. Two doors were fitted and the standard weather equipment was roomy and effective.

The new 60° LTZ and LTWZ JAP side-valves were listed for 1932; the Matchless MX was an added option for 1933 and, from 1934, was the only engine available. The Newport, Monmouthshire Constabulary replaced their motorcycle-sidecar patrols with two Family models in 1933. History does not record if the cars' 60mph top speed, 55mph cruising speed and 44mpg helped reduce Welsh crime figures to any extent.

The arrival of the F4 for the 1934 season edged the Family model towards redundancy; it was discontinued in 1936. These cars are now rare; only seventy-five of the 764 built are known to have survived. Most were driven to destruction and scrapped or converted into more exotic models.

*Above left*: Deco impression of a Sports Family model from the 1935 catalogue. (Morgan Motor Co.)

*Above right*: One of the first three-speeder Family models (1932) with old-style body and brakes, non-detachable wheels and a 60° air-cooled, side-valve JAP. (Author)

*Above left*: Deco impression of a three-speeder Family from the 1935 catalogue. (Morgan Motor Co.)

*Above right*: This 1934 three-speeder Family is powered by a side-valve Matchless MX engine. The cutaway doors are non-standard and alleviate a certain bathtub look from which this model suffered. (Author)

'Can someone help me push this thing?' A hard-worked 1935 Family snapped in Wales in the early 1950s. It has survived and now lives in Paris. (Ken Ellis collection)

## Sports – 1932 to 1939

By 1931 the much-loved but by now rather quaint Aero, which in deference to the feisty Super Aero had become the touring Morgan of choice, was scheduled for replacement. In fond farewell a rare edition of thirty-five three-speed Aeros was built throughout 1932 to supplement the production of twenty-two of the new touring Sports 2-Seaters or Sports models.

Like the other 1932 three-speeders, these early Sports were built on the R chassis with old-style, non-detachable wheels. Though Aero-like at the front, the pretty Sports body was roomier, its gently upswept, curved tail incorporating a stowage locker behind the seats and a flat platform for more luggage above the rear wheel. The front mudguards were of the common, valanced cycle type and any combination of doors could be specified, from none to two. The exhausts ran below the body sides at chassis level. 60° overhead- or side-valve JAP engines were offered.

As with the rest of the range, from 1933 the Sports was built on the D chassis with Dunlop Magnas and the rear bodywork redesigned to house a spare on a flat sloping panel, removable for access to the rear wheel. It did not share the Super Sport's projecting scuttle on the passenger side. In addition to JAP engines, the Matchless MX was offered. In the following year JAPs were withdrawn and Matchless MX2s and MX4s were added to the options.

Whichever engine was fitted, the Sports was a comfortable, attractive and well-appointed tourer with lively performance and commendable economy. The last example was sold to Amal Ltd on 2 December 1938. In total, 428 were built and 134 survive.

Deco impression of the Sports model from the 1935
catalogue. (Morgan Motor Co.)

With a choice
of doors and
extra internal
width, the Sports
was a trifle
more civilised
than the Super
Sports. (Author)

The 1933 Sports
had detachable
wheels and a
spare. This car
was fitted with
a JAP LTOWZ
engine in
preference to
the Matchless
side-valve, which
became optional
in that year.
(Author)

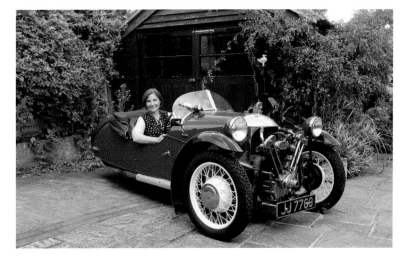

# Super Sports – 1932 to 1939

From time to time an old and ugly rumour resurfaces, asserting that there are more three-speeder Super Sports in circulation today than ever left the Malvern factory. Outrageous? Exaggerated maybe, but look at the figures: of the 820 built, 708 (86 per cent) apparently survive. This seems an extraordinary statistic until the comparative three-speeder Family numbers are considered: 764 built, 75 (10 per cent) remain. Undoubtedly, in the decades after the war, many tired old Family and Sports models, with chassis similar to the Super Sports, metamorphosed into their more desired and valuable siblings.

Only a few obvious features marked the 1932 model from its two-speeder predecessor: the gear-change had moved to the centre of the cockpit and an oil filler now sat on the bonnet behind the radiator cap. Most noticeable, though, was the new 60° LTOWZ JAP engine. Non-detachable wheels, under-body mounted exhausts and the 2½in dropped chassis remained.

The transformation was completed in 1933 when Dunlop Magnas were fitted, the spare being firstly clamped at 45° to the curve of the beetleback, but soon moving to a less precarious horizontal position above the rear wheel. The exhausts ran at high level just

Deco impression of a Super Sports from the 1935 catalogue. (Morgan Motor Co.)

under the cockpit sides, being lowered by 3 inches in 1935 to prevent scorched forearms. During 1934 the beetleback body was phased out in favour of the barrelback, which housed its spare wheel in a recess at the rear. JAP engines, too, took their final bow in that year. A few Matchless MX2s and MX4s found their way into beetlebacks, but from 1935 all the Super Sports were barrel-backed and Matchless-powered. The cars could just reach 70mph, cruise comfortably at 55mph and deliver 40mpg. Braking – never the Morgan's strong point – was much enhanced by the introduction of Girlings in 1938. The last production model was despatched on 23 January 1940, but a further twelve Matchless-engined cars were built from surplus parts in 1946 – nine destined for Australia and three remaining on these shores.

Today, the Super Sports is the most prolific and recognisable of the pre-war three-wheeler Morgans. It embodies the pinnacle of twenty-two years' development of the V-twin-engined cars. In its day it could out-handle, out-accelerate and show a clean pair of heels to most other cars of any class on the road. With its muscular, effortless performance, fabulous sound-track and wicked good looks it still delivers formidable motoring today.

Super Sports barrelback, 1934. (Author)

From 1934 most Super Sports were fitted with Matchless engines. (Author)

# CHAPTER 7

# Morgan F-Types

In 1930, as plans were being laid for the following year's launch of the three-speeders, Morgan's future looked precarious. The Great Depression had been inflicting worldwide economic pain, relentless price-cutting by the mass-producers was rife and sales orders were plummeting. A yet harder truth had to be faced: the Morgan had changed little in its twenty-year life and was now decidedly outdated. Yes, it had its devotees but the noise, smell and vibration of a large V-twin, mediocre braking, primitive transmission and crude weather equipment – the very features which endear the cars to us today – were deterring all but the staunchest of enthusiasts. The three-speeder addressed a few of the old shortcomings but would clearly not deliver the heady sales figures of the mid-1920s. Having once been a mainstream manufacturer, Morgan found itself catering increasingly for a niche market. How ironic that that very niche would become the backbone of its business in future decades. For now, however, HFS had every intention of returning to the mainstream.

A major rethink was required and HFS began to experiment with what was, by his standards, a radically new design. Who knows if, even in 1930, he sensed that the three-wheeler's days were numbered and that he needed to plan for an alternative? It is noteworthy, though, that the characteristics of this new Morgan – its three wheels aside – were closely echoed in the four-wheeled sports cars that followed in 1936 and were to secure the company's future.

Planning progressed over the next three years. The Z-section pressed-steel chassis, which still incorporated the torque tube and tubular front cross-head arrangements of the traditional cars, was designed to accommodate a conventional, small four-cylinder engine, though the existing rear-mounted three-speed gearbox was retained. Despite trials of various engines, none was chosen until 1932 when Ford's Model Y small saloon was launched. Its 933cc 8hp side-valve engine had all the qualities that HFS sought: it was simple, rugged and economical, relatively light and powerful and, best of all, cheap. Once Ford had agreed to supply it in the required numbers the Model F, so-called, was fully configured.

When it arrived there was consternation among the die-hards. Was this really a Morgan? Amusingly, the attitude to change was much the same when the M3W appeared eighty-odd years later, even though it was a good deal closer to the original concept than the F-Types had been.

A note on terminology: Morgan never used the term 'F-Type'. The first model, listed as the Model F, was a four-seater. Later, when the two-seater version appeared, it was listed as the Model F 2-Seater and the Model F became the Model F 4-Seater. The 2-Seater was then superseded by the Model F Super Sports shortened to F Super. The three models were soon known simply as the F4, F2 and F Super by owners and factory alike.

The Ford-powered Morgan was an attempt to modernise the range but, in truth, it did little to halt the decline in sales; 577 were built between 1934 and 1940, and, post-war, a further 253 from 1946 to the end of production in 1952. The F-Type chassis design, however, was a seminal influence on Morgan sports cars for at least sixty years after the three-wheeler's demise.

## Model F, Model F 4-Seater (F4) – 1934 to 1952

Morgan's publicity ahead of the November 1933 Olympia Motor Cycle Show heralded their new ground-breaking, four-cylinder three-wheeler as the last word in performance, comfort and economy. Sensibly hedging their bets, Morgan also stressed that the range of twin-cylinder models would continue in parallel with the new Ford-powered car. The £120 price included full Lucas 6V electrical equipment, all-weather gear and tools. The excitement was a little premature: despatch of the first production cars from Malvern did not start until the following April.

The Model F was a four-seater but, despite having an 8ft 3in wheelbase – 12in longer than the current twin-cylinder Family model – its rear accommodation, as with the Family,

Deco impression of an F4 from the 1935 catalogue. (Morgan Motor Co.)

69

was better suited to children than adults. The 8hp Ford engine sat under a long, louvred bonnet fronted by a handsome, raked, chromed radiator. The body continued rearwards past cycle wings, a squared-off and rather upright windscreen and mildly cut-away doors to a sloping rear-end on which the spare wheel was fixed. With few exceptions, in the first two years the cars were painted Nile Blue with black wings and cream wheels. More daring colour schemes were offered later. Weather equipment comprised a hood and side screens. A De Luxe version, available in 1935 only, provided door pockets, glove boxes and various other minor cosmetic enhancements; twenty-one were sold.

Several elements from the traditional three-wheelers remained: the front sliding-axle suspension and steering, fitted vertically between the two front cross-tubes; the rear-mounted Burman three-speed and reverse gearbox with single chain drive; the Dunlop Magna wheels; the 4ft 2in track. The cable brakes, however, were now operated in unison on all three wheels by pedal, while a ratchet lever applied the rear-wheel brake for parking. A throttle pedal now worked in tandem with the steering-mounted hand-throttle.

Morgans always boasted an excellent power-to-weight ratio, and the Model F was no exception. Weight had been kept below the 8cwt threshold to qualify for £4 road tax, and despite its apparent bulk it could nudge 70mph and cruise at 60mph. Acceleration and hill-climbing were exceptional by contemporary standards and 40mpg was achievable. Precise steering, commendable road-holding and acceptable brakes for its day further enhanced the car's sporting credentials. All this was possible in relative peace and comfort – relative, that is, to the V-twins.

The early wheel-following cycle wings were replaced in late 1934 by graceful, fixed wings flowing back and down to the front corners of the doors. The tail was restyled in 1935 to enclose the spare wheel à la Super Sports. From the 1936 season a more pleasing curved-top windscreen was adopted and the 10hp Ford engine became an option for an extra 7 guineas. The last 8hp engine was fitted to an F4 in January 1948 following which all were 10hp. From 1938 all three Ford-powered models were fitted with the superior Girling brakes, and aluminium bell-housings replaced cast iron. Further minor superficial changes were introduced throughout the four-seater's nineteen-year life.

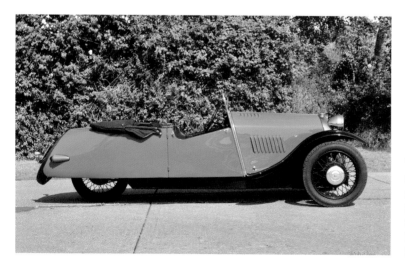

The longer body of the F4 provided more leg room for rear passengers than the old Family models. (Graham Murrell)

The curved windscreen top of this F4 identifies it as post 1936 – 1938 in fact. (Graham Murrell)

The F4 was by far the most popular and long-lived of the F-Types. The old V-twin Family model, which it effectively replaced, was finally dropped in 1936. In the peacetime years between 1934 and 1952, 549 F4s were built, the last one departing Malvern for a Birmingham customer on 25 June. It cost £345 15s (including purchase tax of £75 15s). Of this model 189 (34 per cent) are known to survive.

## Model F 2-Seater (F2) – 1936 to 1938

Sales of the F4 in 1934 and 1935 were, at 155 and eighty-four respectively, disappointing. Many family motorists were opting for the comfort and space of the very cheap, mass-produced small saloons which were available. Nevertheless, HFS had ploughed on with the design of his next car and the Model F 2-Seater made its debut at the November 1935 Olympia Motor Cycle Show, priced at £120 15s for the 8hp. Unlike the F4 launch, deliveries commenced immediately.

Happily, the two-seater body did not inherit its looks from the rather inelegant F4, though it was built on the same chassis. The radiator and bonnet were similar but the treatment around the scuttle and low-cut doors was subtle and stylish, while the tail harmonised nicely with the rest. The effect was enhanced by optional 'Duo' colour schemes that followed the lines of the familiar sweeping wings and added a distinctly deco look. Cycle wings were not an option. The car could be specified with two doors, a passenger door only or no doors, and a fold-flat curved-top windscreen was fitted as standard. The hood was supplied without side screens.

All technical specifications were otherwise similar to the F4. As with the F4 by this time, the car could be fitted with the Ford 8hp engine or, for an additional 7 guineas, the 10hp. About half of F2 customers opted for the latter. Road-holding and performance were much the same as the F4, but the 10hp engine increased top and cruising speeds to 74mph and 65mph respectively and acceleration was markedly more lively.

71

This 1935 F2's 'Duo' colour scheme was available for an extra £2 10s... (Author)

...It flatters the car's already pretty lines. (Author)

The F2 had the shortest production run of the F-Types. It was listed concurrently with the F Super for a year, its original price unchanged, and dropped for the 1939 season. In its three-year life 114 were built, of which sixty-two (54 per cent) have survived.

## Model F Super Sports, F Super – 1938 to 1952

It is not clear why, during the two years following the launch of the smart and sporting Model F 2-Seater, HFS went to the trouble of developing a replacement for it that was, on the face of it, almost identical. However, underlying improvements had been introduced which were major but also subtle, and the Model F Super Sports that emerged for 1938, priced at £136 10s, was a superior and better-looking car. Morgan had reached the zenith of its three-wheeler design – in the twentieth century at any rate – and maybe HFS, now immersed in four-wheeler manufacture, felt that the F Super was a suitable swansong for a line of cars stretching back nearly thirty years. It is known that he personally considered the F-Types to be the pinnacle of his three-wheeler achievements thus far.

The F Super chassis, although built to a similar pattern to the other F-Types, was 4in wider to accommodate a wider body, and afforded a 7ft 11in wheelbase – 4in shorter than the F2/F4 chassis. The body was 2in lower with a correspondingly shorter radiator and low-set headlamps. The track was unchanged at 4ft 2in. Interior comfort was enhanced by the extra body width. Vertical seat adjustment was attainable with Moseley Float-on-Air cushions and the standard passenger door could, if required, be supplemented with another for the driver. The Ford 10hp was the only engine offered. As with the other F-Types now, Girling brakes and a weight-saving aluminium bell-housing were fitted. Cycle wings were initially standard equipment, with the flowing type an option, but from the late 1940s only the latter were available. As with the F2, the car came with the curved-top fold-flat windscreen.

Contemporary road testers, though not always the most reliable or independent of commentators, were unanimously enthusiastic about the F Super. The sporting character and performance of the F2 were now paired with outstanding braking, even better, low-slung good looks and, with the added elbowroom, improved comfort.

In the peacetime years between 1937 and 1952, 167 F Supers were built, of which, amazingly, 107 (64 per cent) are known to survive. The last to leave the factory, priced at £364 18s 4d (including purchase tax of £79 18s 4d) found its new home in Southampton on 29 July 1952.

Swansong. This 1950 F Super was among the last sixty to be built... (Steve Lister)

...Low, dashing and unprotected, here, from an approaching Derbyshire squall. (Steve Lister)

# CHAPTER 8

# Morgan Five-Speeders

For many decades following the demise of the F-Type in 1952, there was little appetite or, indeed, purpose for a three-wheeler revival at Pickersleigh Road. Efforts were focussed on reawakening the market for the four-wheeled Morgan sports cars after the difficult, loss-making years of the post-war depression. The pressure on manufacturers to maximise exports for the good of the economy was unrelenting and by 1960 Peter Morgan, now chairman, had ramped up US sales of the 4/4 and Plus 4 to 85 per cent of total production. A US recession that year suddenly left the company on a financial precipice but, remarkably, he managed to divert sufficient sales to the European and home markets in time to plug the enormous gap. The recession was to last only a year but from the mid-1960s, when tough US safety and emissions legislation began to bite, the export of Morgan cars across the Atlantic became increasingly challenging.

In 2000 Pete Larsen, a specialist sidecar manufacturer in Seattle and devotee of the vintage Morgan three-wheeler, dreamed of designing and manufacturing a modern-day version of it. After ten years of development his vision became reality in the form of the Harley-Davidson-powered Liberty Ace, and a batch of twelve was built in 2009. At that time Morgan were contemplating a return to three-wheelers, not least to benefit from the softer safety and emissions laws applied by the US to motorcycles. Word of Larsen's creation had reached Morgan's top management who were sufficiently interested to visit him in Seattle for a test. They were so impressed with the Ace that talks to buy out all Larsen's designs began there and then. Charles Morgan, the company's chairman, had not been enthusiastic about a return to three-wheelers until, at a late stage, he drove an Ace. He was an instant convert and the deal to acquire Larsen's rights proceeded to completion in early 2010.

Twelve months later a completely, and perhaps hastily, re-engineered version of the Ace was unveiled as the Morgan 3 Wheeler at the 2011 Geneva Motor Show. The original Harley-Davidson engine and Honda transmission had been replaced by S&S power coupled to a five-speed Mazda gearbox and although the car's ancestry was still evident, practically every detail of the Ace had been revised by Morgan in that short period. After a further year of development the first new Morgan three-wheeler model to be seen for sixty years went into production.

# Morgan 3 Wheeler (M3W) – 2012 to 2021

The M3W was a clever impersonation, launched at the height of the retro craze. Painted sensibly – that is without faux bullet-holes, RAF roundels, sharks' teeth or boiler-plate rivets – it could, at a distance and through narrowed eyes, be mistaken for an early 1930s Super Sports or even a late 1920s Super Aero. Despite their marked similarities, however, old and new were very different products of their contrasting eras. In the thrifty 1930s, Morgan aimed to offer a distinctive car of superior performance at a competitive price. In 1932 a young enthusiast with sporting pretensions but limited means would have found the £145 Super Sports a highly seductive and, perhaps with help from the Never Never, narrowly affordable means of everyday transport. The M3W was the offspring of an infinitely more affluent age. Even in 2012 the basic £30,000 price tag seemed a lot for what you got, but by the end of its run in 2021 this could be escalated, with extras, to nearer £50,000. With no weather protection and few creature comforts it was, unashamedly, a toy for the well-heeled with practical, wet-day options on standby in the garage.

The new car's styling was sensational. With its muscular beetleback body and beefy SS Wedge V-twin it looked even more like a Morgan than a Morgan; even the front suspension uprights echoed HFS's fabled sliding axles. Wheelbase and track were 7ft 10in and 5ft respectively. The cockpit was well-finished with plenty of leather and classy, business-like instrumentation. The specification and power-to-weight ratio (160bhp per ton) promised an exhilarating drive. In reality, though, with a 0–60mph time of seven seconds and a top speed of around 115mph, performance was, by modern standards, only brisk after aero-dynamics had taken their toll. The few disappointed punters, however, missed the point and, besides, any shortfall in verve was more than offset by the blasts of wind, exhaust noise and nostalgia. The thrills cost a not-unreasonable 30 miles per gallon overall.

M3W.
Sensational
looks...
(Author)

...from any angle. (Author)

Problems began to emerge early on. Some were insoluble: the weight and bulk of the SS Wedge perched ahead of the front axle line, combined with slender front wheels and tyres, provoked understeer and dictated a wide turning circle and heavy steering at low speeds. The steering geometry made the car skittish on uneven roads, but this was rectified promptly by a redesign. More seriously, fractured chassis tubes near the front suspension mounts were reported in some early cars. Engine vibration was responsible and chassis were thereafter built with thicker-walled tube. Early cush-drives – protecting the gearbox from the engine's characteristic fierce torque spikes – couldn't cope. The CENTA coupling was the third attempt at a remedy and proved successful. By 2014 Morgan had done all they could to cure what was curable.

Despite these major shortcomings and a chronicle of further minor issues, most Morgan 3 Wheeler owners were, and remain, quite as besotted with their cars as the custodians of the vintage cars. Their seemingly inexhaustible patience is testament to both their character and the character of the car, whose obsolescence now guarantees its immortality.

## Super 3 – 2022 On

There was no viable alternative motorcycle engine to replace the S&S Wedge so Morgan, bravely renewing their commitment to the three-wheeler, started afresh and designed a radically new car which incorporates all the cutting-edge manufacturing methods and materials that they have progressively adopted in the production of four-wheelers since the late 1990s. The Super 3, like its predecessor, exists mainly for pleasure but is now better equipped for touring, with more internal space and provision for quantities of luggage. Now the price can be easily pushed, with extras, to over £50,000 and, apart from a tonneau, there is no weather equipment. Most importantly, however, the M3W's worst flaws have been eliminated.

There is barely a shred of Morgan tradition in the construction or appearance of the Super 3: the dashboard is solid ash, and that's it – no coachbuilding, no separate chassis, no V-twin. The inspiration for styling seems to owe much to the movies: the frontal aspect is pure Star Wars, while there is more than a hint of Swallows and Amazons to the rear. The overall look is unusual, modern and not unattractive. Paint and wacky livery options will appeal to a wide spectrum of tastes. Both track and body are 4in wider than the M3W, giving improved road-holding and accommodation. Track and wheelbase measure 5ft 4in and 8ft 3in respectively. The flat exterior 'sideblades' control airflow through the radiators and act as mountings for a range of capacious hard or soft fitted luggage. The roomier cockpit offers superior digital instruments, easily adjustable pedals and steering wheel, a choice of high-quality trims and optional extra stowage.

The turbo-less, three-cylinder 1.5-litre Ford engine is much smoother-running than the S&S Wedge and a gearbox-protecting CENTA coupling is not required. It produces 118bhp (190bhp per ton), 110lbft torque and returns 40 miles per gallon in the Super 3. Despite a 100kg weight handicap over the M3W, quoted 0–60mph time and top speed are around seven seconds and, with an intrepid pilot, 130mph respectively. The slick and much-loved Mazda five-speed gearbox is retained.

The Super 3. (Author)

Weight distribution has been significantly altered by the placement of the relatively short, compact engine behind the front axle line, and purpose-developed Avon tyres now sit on wider 20in alloy wheels. As a result, road-holding and steering have been transformed in this much better balanced car. Understeer has been eliminated, handling is sure-footed and predictable and steering is smoother and lighter. The brakes – never the M3W's strong suit – are much improved and well up to their task.

In the true Morgan tradition, the Super 3 raises smiles wherever it goes and delivers performance, gale-force wind in the hair, a howling exhaust and the sheer joy of seat-of-the-pants driving. It is a worthy new member of the noble Morgan three-wheeler dynasty.

It's in there – somewhere. Under the bonnet of the Super 3. (Author)

A hint of Star Wars. (Author)

# CHAPTER 9

# Morgans in Sport

Lacklustre sales in the months after the launch of the Morgan at Olympia in 1910 called for a promotional rethink. HFS's decision to make an all-out and continuing commitment to motorsport soon brought Morgan cars to public attention and led to the positive sporting image they have projected ever since. The advantages were twofold: sales publicity trumpeted the competition successes and flaunted the speed, stability, reliability and efficiency of the Morgan, while any failures, mechanical or otherwise, were quietly noted and remedied back at Malvern to improve and toughen the breed.

Morgans graduated to most classes of motorsport for which cyclecars were eligible, at club, national and international level. Being robust, light, fast and manoeuvrable, even without modification, they were ideally suited to competition. Trials, record-breaking, track and road racing, all were entered with gusto by the factory and by factory-supported privateers until well into the 1930s, and formidable success rates translated into respectable sales orders. Most motorsport was suspended for the duration of both the wars. Factory involvement in three-wheeler sport was withdrawn in favour of four-wheelers by 1935 but fervent amateurs have continued to race and trial their three-wheelers energetically at club meetings to this day.

This 1929 Super Aero was probably raced at Brooklands. (Author)

# Trials

Trials were introduced in the early 1900s with the object of testing machines in both standard and modified form to their limits – sometimes to destruction. Essentially these were motorcycle competitions that were open to Morgans. There were many types of trial ranging from one-day club events to international six-day marathons. The London–Edinburgh–London, London–Exeter–London and the London–Land's End trials were organised by the Motor Cycle Club and combined long-distance road stages with detours over punishing cross-country sections. The Edinburgh & District Motor Club's Scottish Six Days' Trial and the International Six Days' Trial, staged by the Auto-Cycle Union when held in this country, concentrated on brutal off-road sport. Reliability and efficiency trials were run by the ACU and the Cyclecar Club to test speed, agility, hill-climbing, braking and fuel consumption, initially at the newly opened Brooklands circuit. The hundreds of trials medals won by Morgan competitors in the thirty years up to 1939 provided HFS with an abundance of positive news to fuel his extensive advertising campaigns.

Henry Laird trialling in the mid-1930s. (Alderson collection)

# Record-Breaking

Attempting to set British and World cyclecar speed records was a pastime which few top Morgan drivers could resist, and there was a bewildering array of records to attack: for a range of engine capacities; with or without a passenger; from a flying or standing start; for various distances and times.

In 1912 *Motor Cycling* magazine introduced a trophy for the holder of the 'One Hour' cyclecar record (distance covered in one hour) at the end of each year. On 23 November 1912, HFS covered 59 miles, 1,123 yards in one hour (59.63mph) at Brooklands in a 90-Bore JAP-engined Morgan, setting the British cyclecar record and becoming the first holder of the trophy. Seventeen years and many records later, a JTOR JAP-engined Morgan driven by Gwenda Stewart took the record, again at Brooklands, covering an astonishing 101 miles, 968 yards (101.55mph).

By the 1920s there were few serious challengers to Morgan in the cyclecar class, but the number of British and World records set by JAP- and Blackburne-powered Morgans is nonetheless impressive, with many taken or held in every year of the decade. The introduction of the heavier three-speeders in 1932 and the virtual extinction of the cyclecar as a breed, prompted this class of record-breaking to fade after 1930.

HFS composes himself while his father runs an eye over the Morgan's cockpit prior to the record-breaking 1912 'One Hour' attempt at Brooklands. The Byfleet banking can just be seen to the south. (Alderson collection)

# Racing

British circuit racing up to 1939 can be summed up in one word: Brooklands. When that magnificent triumph of concrete over countryside opened in 1907 it was the only purpose-built motor-racing circuit in Great Britain and the first banked one in the world. Harry Martin, a motorcycle builder, notched up the first ever Brooklands victory for Morgan in 1912 in an international cyclecar race organised by the British Motor Cycle Racing Club in a car powered by a 90-Bore JAP. It was the first of hundreds of Morgan wins there at all levels over the next twenty-seven years. Until its final meeting, four weeks before the outbreak of war in 1939, Brooklands was the undisputed mecca of motorsport in this country. It never opened again for racing.

The lower-key Cadwell Park, Donington Park and Crystal Palace tracks were active from the mid-1930s, but it was not until after the war that British circuits proliferated, many of them developed from RAF airfields.

Arguably Morgan's finest hour in racing was at the 1913 French Cyclecar Grand Prix on a 10-mile road circuit at Amiens which W. G. McMinnies won in a 90-Bore JAP-powered car nearly three minutes ahead of his nearest rival. Afterwards, in a fit of Gallic pique, officials did their best to diminish McMinnies' victory over the second-placed Bédélia by declaring the French car the winning cyclecar and the three-wheeled Morgan merely the winner of the sidecar class. The controversy has rumbled on for over a century, but it was, in truth, a *bravura* result for Morgan both on the track and commercially; sales orders and interest in the cars immediately soared on both sides of the Channel.

Tommy Rhodes dicing with an Austin Seven – both cars nudging the ton on the Brooklands banking in 1934. (Alderson collection)

## Timed Dashes

Sprints and hill climbs, pitting drivers individually against the stopwatch along or up a short stretch of tricky road, have always been popular as an approachable and affordable form of motorsport for the amateur. In early days, closed sections of public road such as the hills at South Harting in West Sussex and Tilburstow in Surrey were used for events, and private tracks such as Shelsley Walsh began to appear. Nowadays owners of both vintage and five-speed Morgans are frequently seen competing at venues across the country.

## HFS the Competitor

In some respects, HFS was an enigma. On one hand he was a talented, imaginative engineer-designer and an apparently hard-nosed entrepreneur, while on the other he was modest, self-effacing and nervous. His expression, seen in some photographs taken before his 1912 record-breaking drive, is a study in terror – unsurprising, perhaps, with the prospect of an hour at full throttle around Brooklands' notoriously uneven *pavé* in a flyweight machine.

He had inaugurated his motorsport campaign with his own gold-medal-winning performance at the first London–Exeter–London Trial in December 1910 in one of his tiller-steered monocars. He had every confidence in his products but, with his competition experience limited to cycle-racing in the old Crystal Palace days and being rather unsure of his own driving abilities at the limit, this achievement was a huge personal boost. It was the first of countless trials successes scored by him with Morgans in subsequent years, many of them shared with Ruth as passenger.

HFS was a gifted driver and competed tirelessly for twenty-five years to promote his cars. Trialling was his forte but he was also a record-breaker and racer, even contesting, albeit unsuccessfully, the 1913 Cyclecar Grand Prix at Amiens. In 1939 he was still representing the factory in four-wheeled Morgans. As the designer and manufacturer

HFS and Ruth tackle Tornapress Hill in an Aero in the 1926 Scottish Six Days Trial. They often wore these striking white outfits when competing. (Alderson collection)

of the cars he campaigned with such success, his contribution to building a proud and enduring reputation for the Morgan name was remarkable and unequalled.

The following group of vignettes describes a few of the significant Morgan racing personalities. There were many more: see also Harold Beart, Cyril Hale, Ronnie Horton, Robin Jackson, Henry Laird and Tommy Rhodes.

## W. G. McMinnies

The motoring writer Gordon McMinnies was doubly influential in Morgan's early fortunes, writing highly pro-Morgan copy in his magazines and landing a breath-taking scoop by winning the 1913 French Cyclecar Grand Prix in a Morgan.

As a young man McMinnies was an experienced and successful motorcycle racer and a journalist on the staff of *Motor Cycling* magazine, writing under the nom de plume of Platinum (a reference to magneto points). On a visit to the 1910 Olympia Show he was impressed by the emerging cyclecar movement's exhibits – particularly the machines displayed on the Morgan stand. He reported enthusiastically in *Motor Cycling* and was soon entrusted by HFS with a runabout to road test for the magazine. The subsequent account could not have been more fulsome and orders for the cars escalated accordingly.

By 1912 McMinnies, now a committed New Motoring supporter, was editing the dedicated magazine *The Cyclecar* and had bought his own Morgan monocar, Jabberwock, which he raced and trialled with success. The contemporary articles he wrote for the two magazines on owning and driving a Morgan make entertaining and fascinating reading for disciples of this early chapter of Morgan and motoring history.

McMinnies' victory in a two-seater Morgan Grand Prix model in the 163-mile 1913 Amiens race was a tour de force. An early tyre repair and a change of faulty plugs were

McMinnies and Thomas return to the paddock in their Grand Prix following the 1913 victory at Amiens. (Alderson collection)

followed in the later stages by a duel with the leading Bédélia after which the Morgan finished three minutes ahead. The contest was written up with *brio* by McMinnies in the next issue of *The Cyclecar* but he modestly attributed his win to meticulous preparation of the car by his mechanic and race passenger, Frank Thomas.

Gordon McMinnies continued to trial and race his Morgans until the outbreak of the First World War when his enthusiasm turned to flying and he trained as an instructor with the Royal Flying Corps. Post-war he returned to a quieter life and resumed his writing with books on flying and travel.

## E. B. Ware

Edward Bradford Ware was a fervent and highly successful entrant of Morgans in races, trials and record-attempts between 1914 and 1924 (excluding the war). He joined J. A. Prestwich's experimental department in 1913 and was supported by JAP in his competition Morgans. In the 1924 Junior Car Club's 200-mile race at Brooklands, Ware and his passenger were seriously injured in a shocking 90mph accident caused by a disintegrated rear tyre. It took both men years to fully recover from their injuries and Ware never competed again. Officialdom deemed Morgans too dangerous to race and they were banned from Brooklands for the next four years.

'Smile please!' Away from the track, E. B. Ware and family pose for a poorly staged publicity shot in a pre-production Family model, *c.* 1920. (Alderson collection)

# H. C. Lones

At work Clive Lones tinkered expertly with power stations. At play it was Morgans. He had been motorcycle-mad in his teens and graduated to Morgans after marrying Nel and qualifying as an electrical engineer. His first, an ancient runabout, was replaced in 1922 by a new side-valve Blackburne-engined Grand Prix, which, after some home-tuning, he entered in a speed trial. It proved surprisingly competitive, and he outpaced all but the top-flight drivers.

Before the war Lones campaigned several Blackburne- and JAP-engined competition Morgans and achieved innumerable wins, records and awards at the highest levels of racing and speed events, often passengered by Nel. He was an ingenious engineer and a skilled tuner and developed the cars continuously to improve speed and handling. The most illustrious and successful of them, the dropped-chassis Super Aero-bodied racer, can be seen, patched and battle-scarred, in the Brooklands Museum today.

After the war Clive Lones pursued 500cc formula racing in cars of his own design and continued hill-climbing into his eighties.

Clive and Nel Lones beam for the cameras after their victory in the 1928 Cyclecar Grand Prix at Brooklands. (Alderson collection)

# Gwenda Stewart and Douglas Hawkes

Gwenda Stewart's life story and dare-devil exploits would have made outlandish reading even in the *Boy's Own Paper*. Born into a distinguished military family and mentioned in despatches in her early twenties while driving ambulances on the Eastern Front in the First World War, she followed a career of racing and record-breaking in cars and on motorcycles throughout the 1920s and 1930s.

In 1924 she and her second husband decamped to France to be close to the Paris Autodrome at Montlhéry which, unlike Brooklands, had no frustrating noise restrictions. From 1927 to 1930 she set most three-wheel cyclecar records, including the 101.55mph 'One Hour', in a Morgan. In 1931 she clocked 118mph at Arpajon in a single-seater Morgan – an all-time three-wheeler record. Later in the decade she graduated to four-wheels, favouring American Derby-Millers and Duesenbergs as her chosen mounts, and went on, among many other achievements, to become the all-time holder of the ladies' Brooklands lap record at 135.95mph in her Derby Special.

Douglas Hawkes was an engineer and a successful racer and record-breaker, driving Morgans in the early 1920s and Bentleys later on. He ran a workshop at the Montlhéry circuit where he met Gwenda in 1930, and was soon designing and preparing her competition cars and partnering her in long-haul record bids.

All Gwenda's husbands were committed to advancing her career and Douglas was no exception. Yes, dear reader, they married in 1937 but this time it was for keeps and after the war they retired to the Greek islands where they sailed the Mediterranean until Douglas's death in 1974. She died in 1990 at the age of ninety-six.

Serious business, record breaking. Gwenda Stewart and Douglas Hawkes at Montlhéry in 1929. (Alderson collection)

# CHAPTER 10

# Morgan Numbers

Personal interests and inclinations differ. Numbers and statistics can either mesmerise or anaesthetise, so, with the exception of a few that are shown in other chapters where relevant, they are confined to this one where they can be relished or bypassed.

## Chassis Numbers

A Morgan's chassis number is a unique identifier that can often be used to establish provenance. The surviving Morgan factory records link post-1928 chassis numbers with the cars' original specifications and despatch details. Altogether, there have been nine series of numbers, their ranges and locations being as follows:

**Two-Speeders**
1 to 15000
Sometimes known as car numbers, they are stamped into the engine timing cover and, rarely, the bevel box.
1A to 2000A
Stamped into the dashboard plaque and, occasionally, the bevel box.
2001B to 2617B
Stamped into the dashboard plaque and, occasionally, the bevel box.
M1 to M674
Stamped into the dashboard plaque and the cast lug connecting the torque tube to the bevel box.

**Three-Speeders**
R1 to R354
Stamped into the dash plaque and the cast lug connecting the torque tube to the gearbox.
D1 to D1895
As for R types.

| MORGAN THREE-WHEELER CHASSIS DATING 1910 TO 1952 | | | |
|---|---|---|---|
| **CHASSIS NUMBER** | **YEAR** | **CHASSIS NUMBER** | **YEAR** |
| 1 to 95 | 1910/11 | M646 to M674 | 1932 |
| 96 to 324 | 1912 | R56 to R354 | 1932 |
| 325 to 743 | 1913 | D1 to D70 | 1932 |
| 744 to 1247 | 1914 | D71 to D748 | 1933 |
| 1248 to 1561 | 1915 | D749 to D1308 | 1934 |
| 1562 to 1786 | 1916 | F1 to F163 | 1934 |
| 1787 to 3187 | 1919 | D1309 to D1558 | 1935 |
| 3188 to 4335 | 1920 | F164 to F247 | 1935 |
| 4336 to 5718 | 1921 | D1559 to D1720 | 1936 |
| 5719 to 7513 | 1922 | F248 to F377 | 1936 |
| 7514 to 8641 | 1923 | D1721 to D1815 | 1937 |
| 8642 to 10189 | 1924 | F378 to F471 | 1937 |
| 10190 to 11501 | 1925 | D1816 to D1862 | 1938 |
| 11502 to 13119 | 1926 | F472 to F526 | 1938 |
| 13120 to 14562 | 1927 | D1863 to D1881 | 1939 |
| 14563 to 15000 | 1928 | F527 to F590 | 1939 |
| 0001A to 1094A | 1928 | D1882 & D1883 | 1940 |
| 1095A to 2000A | 1929 | F591 to F600 | 1940 |
| 2001B to 2080B | 1929 | D1884 to D1895 | 1946 |
| M1 to M31 | 1929 | F601 to F621 | 1946 |
| 2081B to 2517B | 1930 | F622 to F1057 | 1947 |
| M32 to M382 | 1930 | F1058 to F1152 | 1948 |
| 2518B to 2556B | 1931 | F1153 to F1196 | 1949 |
| M383 to M645 | 1931 | F1197 to F1258 | 1950 |
| R1 to R55 | 1931 | F1259 to F1285 | 1951 |
| 2557B to 2617B | 1932 | F1286 to F1301 | 1952 |

Table 1.
(Author)

**F-Types**
F1 to F1301
As for three-speeders and, occasionally, stamped into the chassis cross-member behind the passenger seat.

**Morgan 3 Wheeler and Super 3**
A group of numbers and letters, including a date code, stamped onto the car's VIN plate.

Table 1 links the first seven series of chassis numbers to the year of manufacture. It has been collated from Morgan's surviving production records and other historic evidence.

# Engine and Gearbox Numbers

The JAP engine-numbering system packs copious data into a relatively small space, as Table 2 demonstrates. It is fortunate that, since 85 per cent of the pre-war twin-engined cars were fitted with JAPs, the great majority of owners can benefit from this feast of information. Like most manufacturers, JAP stamped the numbers into the sloping top of the timing chest on the driver's side.

UP TO 1917 JAP gave the 8hp twin engines a serial number - usually of five digits. Then, until 1920, the number was prefixed by a year code as follows:

| M/ or Z/ | 8/ | 9/ | 20/ |
|---|---|---|---|
| 1917 | 1918 | 1919 | 1920 |

TYPICAL 1920-ON JAP numbers with Letters and Numbers LLLLL/L NNNNN/L are explained:

The letters before the first slash: denote engine specifications as follows:

| 1st Letter | Bore mm | Stroke mm | Single cc | Twin cc | 2nd/3rd/4th Letter | |
|---|---|---|---|---|---|---|
| J | 80.0 | 99.0 | 487.0 | 994.0 | T | Twin cylinder |
| K | 85.7 | 85.0 | 490.0 | 980.0 | O | Overhead valve |
| L | 85.7 | 95.0 | 548.0 | 1,096.0 | W | Water-cooled |
| D | 90.0 | 104.0 | 661.0 | 1,323.0 | | |

The 'D' prefix denotes an industrial engine. Some of these were later adapted for Morgans.

| 4th/5th Letter | | So for example: |
|---|---|---|
| Z | Dry sump | KT/ = 980cc twin, sidevalve, air-cooled |
| C | Sports (cyclecar) | KTW/ = 980cc twin, sidevalve, water-cooled |
| S | Sports (motorcycle) | LTOWZ/ = 1,096cc twin, ohv, water-cooled, dry sump |
| R | Racing | JTOR/ = 994cc twin, ohv, air-cooled, racing |

The letter after the first slash: denotes the year of manufacture as follows:

| P | N | E | U | M | A | T | I | C | S |
|---|---|---|---|---|---|---|---|---|---|
| 1920 | 1921 | 1922 | 1923 | 1924 | 1925 | 1926 | 1927 | 1928 | 1929 |

| W | H | Y | Z | D | R | V | F | O | G |
|---|---|---|---|---|---|---|---|---|---|
| 1930 | 1931 | 1932 | 1933 | 1934 | 1935 | 1936 | 1937 | 1938 | 1939 |

These date codes were then repeated for the years 1940 to 1959.

The number: generally five digits, this is the engine's unique factory serial number.

Letter codes following the serial number and final slash: there are many of these, usually relating to minor variations in, for instance, standard bearing size or piston type.

Table 2. (Author)

Other engine-makers were not so helpful, but the received wisdom on numbering is as follows:

- The water-cooled British Anzani engines fitted to Morgans were numbered CCW/ up to number 1689 until 1925 and M3/ from number 1690 thereafter.
- Blackburne engines fitted to Morgans were all numbered sequentially, regardless of type, with the prefixes KMA, KMC, VCM or ZCM (see Chapter 4).
- The two common MAG engine types were numbered 2C13A (air-cooled) and 2C20A (water-cooled) followed by a five-digit serial number.
- Matchless engines were numbered MX/501 to 1166 (side-valve, water-cooled), MX2/500 to 734 (overhead-valve, air-cooled) and MX4/500 to 975 (overhead-valve, water-cooled). They were fitted to Morgans between 1933 and 1939 so it is possible to approximate the year of an engine's manufacture from its number by using simple arithmetic.
- Side-valve Ford engine numbers comprised five or six digits prefixed by Y (8hp) or C (10hp) stamped into the block.
- The Burman-type gearboxes fitted to Morgans from 1932 to 1952 were stamped with a number on the apex of the rear arched section of the casing. Typically, a two-, three- or four-digit number is prefixed by R (first series, twins), MR (modified R, twins) and MA or XC (F-Types), but the prefixes sometimes vary. Gearbox numbers can often help to identify a car or chassis.

# Production Numbers

Table 3 shows production numbers from 1910 to 1952. Morgan records tracked the progress of a car through the factory from receipt of a customer's order when a chassis number was allocated, through manufacture to despatch. The table has been collated from surviving production records and other historic evidence.

Factory records for the five-speeder Morgan Three-Wheeler are not available but the Morgan Motor Company quotes around 2,500 as the total output from 2012 to 2021, of which about 2,000 were built in the first five years. Thereafter sales dropped sharply, possibly over worries about reliability, until fewer than one per week was being built in the two years leading up to the end of production.

At the time of writing, Super 3 numbers are unknown.

### MORGAN THREE-WHEELER
#### CARS PRODUCED 1910 TO 1952

| YEAR | TWINS | F-TYPES | TOTAL | YEAR | TWINS | F-TYPES | TOTAL |
|---|---|---|---|---|---|---|---|
| 1910/11 | 95 | - | 95 | 1931 | 324 | - | 324 |
| 1912 | 229 | - | 229 | 1932 | 458 | - | 458 |
| 1913 | 419 | - | 419 | 1933 | 676 | - | 676 |
| 1914 | 504 | - | 504 | 1934 | 544 | 155 | 699 |
| 1915 | 314 | - | 314 | 1935 | 229 | 84 | 313 |
| 1916 | 225 | - | 225 | 1936 | 167 | 127 | 294 |
| 1917/18 | NO PRODUCTION | | | 1937 | 94 | 75 | 169 |
| 1919 | 1,401 | - | 1,401 | 1938 | 51 | 70 | 121 |
| 1920 | 1,148 | - | 1,148 | 1939 | 19 | 63 | 82 |
| 1921 | 1,383 | - | 1,383 | 1940 | 2 | 7 | 9 |
| 1922 | 1,795 | - | 1,795 | 1941/45 | NO PRODUCTION | | |
| 1923 | 1,128 | - | 1,128 | 1946 | 11 | 16 | 27 |
| 1924 | 1,548 | - | 1,548 | 1947 | - | 26 | 26 |
| 1925 | 1,312 | - | 1,312 | 1948 | - | 54 | 54 |
| 1926 | 1,618 | - | 1,618 | 1949 | - | 48 | 48 |
| 1927 | 1,444 | - | 1,444 | 1950 | - | 62 | 62 |
| 1928 | 1,510 | - | 1,510 | 1951 | - | 27 | 27 |
| 1929 | 996 | - | 996 | 1952 | - | 16 | 16 |
| 1930 | 778 | - | 778 | | | | |
| | | | | TOTALS | 20,422 | 830 | 21,252 |

Table 3. (Author)

# Survivors

Table 4 compares a 2020 census of survivors with the total numbers of cars produced. Where known, the model-by-model survival figures of earlier cars are given in Chapters 5 to 7. It is too early to establish numbers for the M3W and Super 3, however it is safe to assume that the great majority have survived.

### MORGAN THREE-WHEELER
#### PRODUCTION/SURVIVAL RATES

| | 2-Speeders 1910-1932 | 3-Speeders 1932-1946 | F-Types 1934-1952 | TOTAL |
|---|---|---|---|---|
| Cars built | 18,229 | 2,193 | 830 | 21,252 |
| Known Survivors | 469 | 962 | 358 | 1,789 |
| Survival Rate | 2.6% | 43.9% | 43.0% | 8.4% |

Table 4. (Author)

# Prices

Table 5 shows the average basic price of a Morgan excluding extras and engine upgrades.

By comparison, a basic Austin Seven was priced about £25 higher between 1923 and 1928. The price gap narrowed until 1931, after which the Morgan became the dearer car by around £10. By 1938 they were similarly priced.

Upgrades from air-cooled to water-cooled side-valve engines cost around £10, while an overhead-valve JAP or Blackburne was about £15 more than a side-valve.

Prices of typical 1929 Morgan extras are shown in Table 6.

**MORGAN THREE-WHEELER**
**AVERAGE BASIC PRICES 1910 TO 1952**

| Year | £ | Year | £ | Year | £ | Year | £ |
|---|---|---|---|---|---|---|---|
| 1910/11 | 89 | 1922 | 189 | 1932 | 119 | 1946 | 289* |
| 1912 | 89 | 1923 | 157 | 1933 | 111 | 1947 | 305* |
| 1913 | 89 | 1924 | 132 | 1934 | 117 | 1948 | 325* |
| 1914 | 95 | 1925 | 120 | 1935 | 117 | 1949 | 335* |
| 1915 | 95 | 1926 | 116 | 1936 | 114 | 1950 | 345* |
| 1916 | 95 | 1927 | 109 | 1937 | 117 | 1951 | 356* |
| 1917/18 | n/a | 1928 | 112 | 1938 | 128 | 1952 | 367* |
| 1919 | 138 | 1929 | 107 | 1939 | 130 | | |
| 1920 | 184 | 1930 | 106 | 1940 | 130 | | |
| 1921 | 217 | 1931 | 107 | 1941/45 | n/a | | |

*Includes purchase tax @ 28%

Table 5.
(Author)

**MORGAN THREE-WHEELER**
**EXTRAS AVAILABLE FOR 1929**

Where not included in Specification, and if ordered with machine.

| | £ | s. | d. |
|---|---|---|---|
| Lucas Electric Starter | 8 | 0 | 0 |
| Hood Covers | | 15 | 0 |
| Side Screens (De Luxe and Family) | 1 | 15 | 0 |
| Speed Indicator | 3 | 10 | 0 |
| Clock, Dashboard | 2 | 0 | 0 |
| Stork Mascot | | 7 | 6 |
| Aluminium Number Plates | | 17 | 6 |
| Painting Numbers | | 5 | 0 |
| Newton Front Wheel Shock Absorbers, to Models other than the Super-Sports | 2 | 15 | 0 |
| Standard Colours - Dark Blue or Panhard Red. | | | |
| Other Colours      ...      ...      ... extra | 2 | 0 | 0 |
| Chassis Colours   ...      ...      ...    " | 1 | 0 | 0 |
| Bodies painted Two Colours   ...   " | 2 | 10 | 0 |
| Special Colour Upholstery   ...   " | 1 | 0 | 0 |

Table 6.
(Author)

# CHAPTER 11

# Morgans Today

## Driving

There are few pleasures to match a stint at the wheel of a Morgan three-wheeler. All are a delight to drive and most – unlike much pre-war porridge – have surprisingly brisk performance for their size and class and can hold their own on modern roads, though motorways are not recommended. Five-speeders are rather more lively and benefit, too, from adequate brakes. All Morgans are wonderfully noisy.

A current worry is the Great British pothole – obviously, three-wheelers are at a 50 per cent disadvantage over four-wheeled cars in their ability to avoid them. The very limited vertical travel in the front suspension makes an inadvertent coming-together with one of these destructive horrors a painfully jarring experience. Detachable wheels and spares

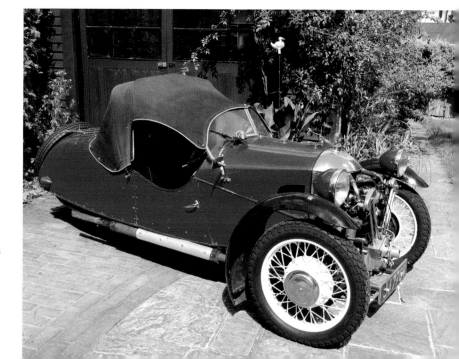

Deployment of weather equipment on a Morgan severely restricts vision from within. (Author)

only arrived in 1933; older cars' punctures have to be repaired somehow at the roadside. Front-wheel brakes were standardised in 1927 and geared steering in 1929. A muscular right leg, strong shoulders and a heightened sense of anticipation are, therefore, essential when conducting the more primitive cars. In truth, braking was barely adequate before the three-speeder era.

Cold, wet weather can be unpleasant – dangerous, even, for the early cars whose band brakes become quickly water-logged and ineffective. Weather equipment when deployed on the V-twins reduces vision to near-zero, works reasonably well on F-types, and is unavailable for five-speeders.

## Maintaining

Old Morgans repay a little upkeep with an admirable degree of reliability and economy. Indeed, considering most survivors are approaching their first centenary and were never built to last beyond a decade, it is extraordinary how seldom the well-maintained ones go wrong – testament to their sound design and quality of manufacture, not to mention the loving care of their custodians.

Naturally, few have endured the ravages of many decades without some major restoration work. At worst, complete chassis, body and engine rebuilds can still be undertaken by specialists and there are very few components, major or minor, that cannot be either sourced from the Morgan Three-Wheeler Club, made by an expert engineer or found second-hand. The Morgan is simple and lightweight – even the engine can, with care, be lifted solo – and most routine work can be undertaken by a sympathetic owner with a reasonable level of mechanical competence.

Liberal use of the oil-can and grease-gun is a must. Regular lubrication of the sliding axles, steering mechanism, wheel-bearings, clutch and control linkages, bevel box or gearbox, rear fork, and chains, sprockets and dogs is straightforward – all are easily accessible. Checks on oil, water and fuel levels and tyre pressures should be carried out before a trip.

Few would dare to interfere with the intricacies of twenty-first-century cars like the M3W and Super 3. Beyond checking fluid levels and tyres, maintenance is probably best left to a Morgan agent.

## Buying

A very old car can suffer significant identity change over an eighty- or ninety-year life – sometimes through economic necessity, sometimes for economic gain. Morgans, whose chassis, bodies and engines are so easily interchangeable, have been particularly prone to this.

In the aftermath of the war, when cheap transport was scarce, discarded Morgan remains were pressed back into service with makeshift repairs and patched-up bodywork. Later, when the cars began again to be properly appreciated, opportunists soon spotted that a humble Family or Sports model, for example, was ripe for conversion to a more precious Super Sports or an F4 to an F2 for similar motives. Morgans with originality and provenance command a premium.

Inexperienced buyers should be aware of the pitfalls to avoid disappointment and disenchantment and ensure that they fully understand a car under consideration. Thorough preliminary homework and MTWC membership are recommended; seasoned MTWC members are generally available and willing to give informal help and advice on condition and originality.

## The Morgan Three-Wheeler Club

For anyone involved with Morgan three-wheelers, from the mildly curious newcomer to the obsessive collector, membership of the MTWC is indispensable. It is regarded worldwide as one of the most comprehensive and supportive of the single-make car clubs. Owners of all models, ancient and modern, are welcome, but ownership of a Morgan is not a prerequisite to joining.

MTWC members explore a watermill after a languid pub lunch and a gentle 'run' along country lanes. (Author)

Members can take advantage of the many benefits the club has to offer, such as *The Bulletin*, a first-rate monthly magazine crammed with fascinating articles covering all the cars and including the eagerly followed 'Floggery' section; Mogspares, which supply a huge range of parts for most models at the lowest possible prices; access to technical support and buying advice; insurance valuations; help for aspiring young owners; a gateway to competitive events for more spirited drivers; current news and almost unlimited Morgan knowledge on the website – mtwc.co.uk – much of which is available to non-members.

The club's social activities are spread across twenty local British groups and a further six worldwide. Every member is welcome at all meetings and events. Each group generally holds a pub meeting at least once per month. Veteran members, often found at these meetings, are usually more than happy to share their wisdom and experience with new recruits.

If you are not already a member of the Morgan community and now feel ready to take matters a stage further – to perhaps join the club or even start looking for a car – be warned, it could be life-changing. Good luck!

'The Pioneer – & Still the Best!' (Sue Clark)